PENGUIN HANDBOOKS

PASTA AND NOODLES

Merry White is a graduate of Harvard University where she read Asian sociology. For a year she prepared once-a-week lunches for a crowd of scholars and their guests at Harvard's Center for West European Studies and now does freelance catering for large groups. Merry White has a small daughter and has travelled extensively in Europe, Africa and Asia. She has also written *Cooking for Crowds*, published in Penguins.

MERRY WHITE

PASTA AND NOODLES

Illustrations by Edward Koren

PENGUIN BOOKS

Penguin Books Ltd, Harmondsworth, Middlesex, England
Penguin Books, 625 Madison Avenue, New York, New York 10022, U.S.A.
Penguin Books Australia Ltd, Ringwood, Victoria, Australia
Penguin Books Canada Ltd, 2801 John Street, Markham, Ontario, Canada L3R 1B4
Penguin Books (N.Z.) Ltd, 182–190 Wairau Road, Auckland 10, New Zealand

—

First published in the U.S.A. as *Noodles Galore* by Basic Books, Inc., 1976
Published in Penguin Books 1979
Copyright © Basic Books, Inc., 1976

—

—

Made and printed in Great Britain by
Richard Clay (The Chaucer Press) Ltd,
Bungay, Suffolk
Set in Monotype Plantin

For Jenny

ACKNOWLEDGEMENTS

More people than I can possibly mention here have helped with this book. One who did more than help, however, and whose name should be on the title page, is my husband, Lew Wurgaft, who did the research, testing, eating, and typing for many of the recipes, and who is even now cheerfully planning our next noodle dish.

My parents also deserve more than a line for their support and help, in this as in everything.

However, I especially want to thank those who have so generously given me their recipes, who have gathered up strands of their noodle heritage and presented them to me. Frank Phillips, Carol and Lynn Karlson, Dick Chen. Trin Yarborough, Tom Gold, Leslie Blumberg, Judith Strauch, Beatriz Bloom, Steve Kapos and Lisa DeFrancis, I thank here.

Farrell Wallerstein, my editor and friend, has been a great encouragement and thoughtful guide. And the prospect of doing this book with Ed Koren has been a constant source of cheer. The drawings are, as ever, a delight.

CONTENTS

INTRODUCTION

There is no staple food of human invention as varied and as wide-spread as the noodle. Noodles appear in virtually every culture, in a dazzling profusion of shapes, and in a surprising variety of cooking styles. While we tend to think first of Italian pasta, we should also note that noodle dishes are a commonplace of Asian cuisine. And they appear elsewhere as well, in such exotic forms as sweet corn-flour noodles served with syrup and rosewater ice cream from India, fiery hot soup noodles from Tibet, and an amazing assortment of 'fast-food' noodle snacks from Japan. In the pages that follow I will, of course, draw on the more familiar 'mainstream' of noodle cookery, but just as often I will draw on the more esoteric noodle traditions that particularly appeal to me.

The principal reason, of course, for the universality of the noodle is its economy. Traditionally, noodles have served as an alternative staple food in many parts of the world. We in the West may have a wider choice of foods, but noodles can provide us with a nourishing and inexpensive staple as well. We should, in fact, learn from cultures where economy is a necessity to limit our intake of meat protein. In Asia, for instance, meat, vegetables, and eggs are often used as garnishes for grains and grain products, rather than vice versa. We may not wish to go as far as that, but with a small amount of meat (between 8 oz (250 g) and 1 lb (500 g)) you can serve six people a filling and nutritious main course. And, as our section on vegetable dishes will show, it is possible to plan interesting and satisfying meatless meals using noodles as a base.

However practical a food the noodle may be, its history is embroidered with romance and mythology. Among the 'myths of origin', the most popular one revolves around Marco Polo's trip to the Orient in the 1270s. Among the treasures he brought back with him, the noodle is said to have had the most importance. Yet the existence of the noodle in Italy predated his trip, for rules governing the size and shape of noodles existed there as early as 1200. It is also said that his reports of Chinese noodles used already existing Italian words for these foods, and didn't involve neologisms. And yet the tradition serves a useful symbolic purpose, for it ties together, however apocryphally, the two greatest noodle-making cultures, the Italian and the Chinese. The issue of who was first (and the Chinese, during an archaeological excavation, recently discovered a petrified prehistoric noodle dumpling) belongs as much to the world of 'politics' as it does to the history of food.

As we have already suggested, it is hard to find a culture that does not use some form of noodle, whether borrowed long ago and assimilated, or added to the diet recently, in a still self-conscious adaptation. The Chinese 'great tradition' spread through Southeast Asia and Japan, and westward through Burma, India and the Middle East, where it meets the easternmost fringe of the European noodle. In many Asian societies, rice culture exists side by side with wheat culture, and noodles are often made from rice, soya beans, potatoes, and other substances as much as from wheat.

European noodles take their style from Italy, but also from a later and more robust tradition, the fresh noodles of Middle Europe – as, for instance, German dumplings, Czech spaetzle, and Jewish noodle puddings. Argentinian noodle dishes, too, are influenced by the Germans, as well as by the Italians. And American noodle dishes are hybrids as well – Chicago chow mein, spaghetti with meat sauce and macaroni cheese.

All of these cultural cross-currents stimulate a cook's imagination. Besides tasting good and being economical, noodles are wonderful for their versatility. I often buy the day's nicest, cheapest, most seasonal produce, a bit of meat or fish, and a pound (500 g) of noodles whose shape has caught my eye. Armed with no recipe but with a knowledge of the properties of the ingredients, I can produce an interesting meal quickly. Noodles are a great liberator, and the recipes in these pages will give you some ideas of how and where to begin.

There is a special magic for me in watching noodles being made. The places themselves are wonderful. An Italian pasta factory, even a small one producing an impoverished sixty varieties out of the possible six hundred now made in Italy, is a combination of traditional lore (what shapes at what seasons, who is entrusted with the old family pasta dough recipe, and so forth) and technical efficiency. After contemplating a small glass case filled with samples of sizes and shapes, you order by weight, shape, and size. Then you watch as an old woman in black feeds a perfectly kneaded and flattened sheet of dough into an enormous contraption, surely a relic of the industrial revolution, and gives the handle five healthy turns to produce a tray of beautiful, floury ribbons of tagliatelle. Or, if you are lucky, it is the day on which tortellini are made, and she places a pound or two, dusted with cornmeal and flour, lovingly into a box, with rapid-fire directions about cooking them.

Pasta secca (dried noodles) are sold in fascinating varieties in grocers. If you are not bound by the traditions of what pasta to serve with what sauce, then a choice becomes an exercise in whimsy or aesthetic taste. An artist friend bought her husband a birthday gift of about forty varieties of noodles, whose wonderful names – lumache ('snails'), fusilli ('twists'), gemelli ('twins'), farfallette ('little butterflies'), and so on – appeal as much as the shapes.

In some cultures noodles have a sacred as well as a dietary function. Near the town of Pokhara in Nepal I saw brilliantly coloured swirls of translucent rice noodles laid out to dry in the sun on deep green banana leaves. As I later learned, they served as both food and offerings to the gods. In other places pasta has been used for purely decorative purposes – dyed, painted, and lacquered into necklaces and pictures. At least the painted Nepali noodles were offerings for gods to *eat*.

NOODLE DEFINITIONS

In writing this book, I have encountered some difficult problems of definition. Just what is a noodle, and what is not? Simply for the purpose of keeping this project manageable, I have decided that any flour paste that is boiled or cooked in liquid and has certain recognized shapes, or categories of shape, is a noodle. Nonetheless, I have included certain 'noodles' that don't fit, and left out some which do. For instance, though I have included a few Italian stuffed pasta dishes, I have not included absolutely delicious comparable Chinese stuffed noodle dough pastries. Such foods as *shiu mai*, 'Peking ravioli', bean paste dumplings, and shrimp balls are among my favourite foods, but, like the Italian tortellini and capelletti, they are somewhat difficult to make well. I admit to yielding to laziness, and when I can I prefer to eat them professionally, though freshly, made.

In addition, there is a group of recipes that I enjoy making, but that do not completely fit my 'definition' of noodles. These I have called 'near noodles', since they are a little more than dumpling, if less than macaroni; these recipes appear at the end of the book.

NOODLE NUTRITION

Noodles are made of many substances, with varying nutritional worth. Yet even the simplest wheat flour and water noodle has more protein and carbohydrates than potatoes, and, since noodles are often served in sauces containing some combination of vegetable, cheese, or meat, the nutritional balance is very good.

Some years ago, a Maryknoll priest working in Hong Kong

invented a recipe that could utilize surplus foods in a very high protein noodle. He set up a factory producing 7,000 lb (3,500 kg) of noodles a day made from 5 per cent powdered milk, 20 per cent corn meal, and 75 per cent wheat flour. This kind of noodle can be made at home, with various high protein flours, and you can experiment with vegetable additions as well (cooked, and liquidized).

An important nutritional aspect of noodles is their catalytic property in combination with vegetable protein, a phenomenon that has attracted attention recently. Roughly, the idea is that certain starches, such as rice and wheat flour, produce the effect of heightening, 'stretching' the protein content of certain vegetable proteins found in legumes such as beans. Thus Mexican rice and beans, and Nepali rice and lentils (*dahl baht*) are nutritionally reasonably well balanced. Thus, too, the perfect noodle meal: *pasta e fagioli*.

Recently, athletes have been encouraged to eat pasta before performing, since it both provides a burst of energy and, unlike sugar 'boosters', sustains the energy over a long period of time. Of course, no athlete would devour a large plate of spaghetti and meatballs before the Big Game, but I can imagine eating a helping of small macaroni, tossed with yogurt, spring onions, and freshly ground pepper, and then climbing a small mountain . . .

These nutritional discoveries seem to invalidate the arguments against pasta put forth in the twenties and thirties by the Italian Futurists, a group of artists and poets who were engaged in revolutionizing every aspect of Italian society. They were especially interested in food and produced a cookery book (*La Cucina Futurista*), which includes a polemic against pasta. In their own way, they were romantics of the machine age, and idolized speed. They wrote 'aeropoetry' and made dishes of meat resembling rocket ships.

Thus the ideal men were '*agili, desti, veloci, elettrici, furibondi*', and their diet had to conform to the new style of life. F. T. Marinetti, often the spokesman for the group, saw a future where food was only the medium for a kinaesthetic experience, and where nutrition came in pill form, taken daily. When eaten, meals were to be light, the inspiration, not the inhibitor of action. Marinetti saw pasta as the enemy of the new, sinewy, heroic warrior-Italian, whose brain would be slowed as well as his body, and whose virility could be greatly threatened, by a dish of spaghetti.

Though pasta may have been the enemy of the Futurists, it is the friend of our present need for a balanced, inexpensive diet. And the Italian varieties of pasta are not the only alternative. The following pages will try to suggest the amazing variety of ways in which noodles are made and cooked throughout the world.

NOODLE TYPES

One of the purposes of this book is to introduce you to the enormous variety of Asian noodle recipes, as well as to the many delicious Western noodle dishes. I'll begin with some basic Asian noodle types, available wherever there is a Chinese or other Asian grocer.

Bean thread noodles. These are both Chinese and Japanese. They are thin, translucent noodles that are used simmered in soups or soaked in hot dishes, and used in *mizutaki* and in Chinese hot-pot dishes. They are made from the mung bean, from which most bean sprouts are made. The Japanese name for them is *shirataki*.

Cellophane or vermicelli noodles. These are usually made from seaweed, and are very fine, translucent noodles. They are used as above, particularly in cold dishes.

Phaluda. One of the few indigenous Indian noodles, these are made from cornflour paste and served cold with syrup and rosewater ice cream (*kulfi*) or fruit.

Potato starch noodles. Used like bean thread noodles (*see above*).
Rice sticks and rice chips. Chinese and Southeast Asian noodles used stir-fried, soaked, and simmered, but especially deep-fried. When tossed in hot oil, they puff up and increase about six times in volume and become very light and crisp. Rice sticks are long thin noodles, while rice chips, as the name suggests, come in small chips.
Shrimp noodles. These Southeast Asian noodles are made from shrimp paste mixed with wheat flour.
Soba. Made from buckwheat flour, and slightly greenish in colour, this is the most popular Japanese noodle. The noodle restaurants that are all over Japan provide soba with every sort of garnish, from eel to ice cubes and chopped ham. These noodles are, also, part of Japanese social ritual, for when a newcomer enters his new home the neighbours on each side present him with soba noodles. These are to point out the closeness of their future relationship by punning on the word soba, which also means 'next to' or 'beside'.
Somen. A thin Japanese wheat vermicelli, used in soups and in cold noodle dishes.
Udon. A Japanese wheat noodle, the thickest of Japanese noodles. Used in cold and hot noodle dishes.
Wheat or egg and wheat noodles. These are sold fresh or dry, but are much the best fresh. Chinese egg noodles come both wide and narrow; the wheat noodles are usually flat. Substitute spaghetti for them if you cannot find them fresh. You can package fresh noodles in plastic and freeze them almost indefinitely, so, once you have found a supplier of fresh Chinese noodles, you are well set.

Italian pasta is so rich in variety, and poetic in names, that it is hard to make a selection. The following is thus only a very partial list of some of the types you may be able to buy in this country.

One interesting fact is that Italian pasta is divided roughly into two main varieties, and these have a definite geographical distribution: northern noodles are flat ribbons of various widths; southern pasta is tubular.

Whenever possible, where fresh pasta is unavailable, buy imported Italian pasta.

Cannelloni. Large tubes of pasta for stuffing, often covered in sauce before baking. Parboil before using, as with other large stuffable pasta like lasagne or big shells.

Lasagne. Wide flat pasta, used layered with vegetables, meat, and cheese, or sometimes rolled with a filling and covered with sauce before baking. Parboil before using.

Tagliatelle. Long flat ribbons of pasta, known in Rome as fettucine. Technically, tagliatelle is $\frac{1}{8}$ inch (3 mm) wider than fettucine, but for cooking purposes they are interchangeable.

The following are all interesting shapes of macaroni, or thicker noodles. Ziti, gemelli and mafalda are long; the rest are usually less than 2 inches (5 cm) long – though shells can be bigger than that.

Conchiglie

Farfalle

Fusilli

Gemelli

Macaroncini curvi

Mafalda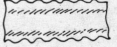

Penne

Rigatoni

Rotini

Ziti

The following are small noodles, useful in soups or buttered in place of rice, or in cheese dishes:

Orzo

Stellini

Acini di pepe

Ditalini

Small macaroni

Alphabets

There are obviously hundreds more – do your own local survey.

Noodles have been satisfactorily exploited by a burgeoning health food industry. Health food shops have interesting varieties of noodles, which you should try with the warning that some are quite fragile, when cooked, because of the low-gluten flours they contain. Undercook them slightly.

A note on portions of pasta: many commercial American noodles give suggested numbers of servings per pound on the package. Two ounces (60 g) dry pasta per serving is the size most often given. I find this is quite inadequate, especially for a main-course pasta dish, and recommend 1 lb (500 g) of pasta for four to six people, depending on the meal and the other ingredients of the dish. If a simple dish like spaghetti with *pesto* is being served as a main course, six people would probably require 2 lb (1 kg) of spaghetti. All the recipes in this book are designed for six servings.

HOMEMADE NOODLES: SOME BASIC RECIPES

There are some recipes in this book that specify the use of homemade (or fresh from a factory) noodles. I strongly suggest that you try making them at least *twice*. The first time will seem like work, the second will seem more fun and more natural. The product of both will be noodles so delicious they'll seem like a new sort of food altogether. And look for local noodle makers – Italian, Chinese,

German, whatever – whose noodles you can buy fresh. You can freeze fresh noodles, in plastic bags, for months.

Although not exhaustive, this section will give you a few basic recipes and instructions for making several types of noodles. Each recipe yields approximately 1½–2 lb (750 g–1 kg) of noodles.

Fresh Pasta

This pasta is made without eggs, and it takes less rolling, and is easier to work than egg pasta. However, it dries out quickly and must be kept under cloths while it is being used. It can be used both for noodles and for stuffed pasta.

2 oz (60 g) butter
8 oz (250 g) unbleached white
   flour, preferably semolina flour
2 pinches of salt

Boiling water as needed to make
   a stiff dough (usually less than
   ½ pint (250 ml)

Put the butter and flour in a mixing bowl and mix together with your fingers. Add the salt and just enough boiling water to make a stiff dough, then knead until smooth.

Divide the dough into two parts and let it rest under a cloth on a board for 30 minutes.

If you are using a pasta machine, proceed as on page 26. If you are making your pasta by hand, roll each half of the dough out, as thin as possible, on a floured board. (Make sure you have a big enough board before you start, or use a clean tabletop.) Turn the dough as you roll it out, and flour it well. For cutting and cooking the pasta, see pages 25–8.

Fresh Egg Pasta

This pasta is good for tagliatelle and other flat noodles, and for cannelloni, lasagne, and tortellini. Use semolina flour if you can get it – but be sure it's the *flour*, not the fine-grained semolina cereal.

1 lb (500 g) unbleached white
    flour, preferably semolina flour
1 tablespoon warm water

1 teaspoon salt
3 whole eggs plus 1 egg yolk

Sift the flour on to a large board or tabletop, then make a well in the middle. Combine the water and salt to dissolve the salt, and place in the well with the eggs and the yolk. Gradually mix the flour into the liquids, then knead thoroughly to make a smooth, firm dough. Add more water, if necessary, or, if dough is sticky, knead hard and, if necessary, add more flour. Make into a ball, wrap in a clean cloth, and let stand for at least 1 hour.

Divide the dough into four pieces and roll into balls. On a floured surface, roll out each piece into a very thin circle ($\frac{1}{16}$ to $\frac{1}{8}$ inch (2–3 mm) thick). Place on clean cloths and dry for 45 minutes.

If you are using a pasta machine, proceed as on page 26. If you are making your pasta by hand, proceed as on page 25.

Pasta Verde (Spinach Noodles)

This can also be made with fresh spinach, washed, picked over, and cooked in the water clinging to its leaves until wilted.

8 oz (250 g) unbleached white flour, preferably semolina flour
2 eggs
½ teaspoon salt

8 oz (250 g) frozen spinach, thawed, squeezed dry, and chopped very fine

Combine all the ingredients, then add just enough warm water, bit by bit, to make a firm, elastic dough.

Form the dough into a ball and let it rest on a board for 1 hour, covered with a clean cloth.

If you are using a pasta machine, proceed as on page 26. If you are making your pasta by hand, proceed as on page 25.

Soya Bean Noodles

1 lb (500 g) soya flour
1 teaspoon salt
2 egg yolks

Combine all the ingredients with enough cold water to make a soft but firm dough. Roll in waxed paper and set aside for 2 hours in the refrigerator.

If you are using a pasta machine, proceed as on page 26. If you are making your own pasta, roll out and cut the dough as described on page 25. Then drop the noodles into boiling salted water for 5 minutes.

MODELLING THE NOODLES

By Hand

Prepare the dough according to your recipe. Let it stand for the required amount of time, then:

For regular noodles: Roll out the dough on a floured tabletop or board as thin as you can can, turning constantly and adding more flour as needed. Roll the dough up into a swiss roll shape, then flour a sharp knife and cut across into thin coils of noodles, $\frac{1}{8}$ inch (3 mm) wide or whatever width you want. Immediately open up the noodles and dry them on clean cloths or a floured surface, or toss them immediately into boiling, salted water and cook according to the directions on page 28.

For stuffed pasta: Roll out the dough on a floured tabletop or board as thin as you can. Cut with a sharp, floured knife into whatever size pieces are required (rectangles for cannelloni, or lasagne, or whatever) and dry as above before using. Always let pasta dry slightly before stuffing.

By Machine

Prepare the dough according to your recipe and let it stand for 30 minutes to 1 hour, covered. If your machine has not been used before, run a piece of flour and water dough through, according to the manufacturer's directions, before using. This will remove any dirt or oil in it.

Using the side of the machine for kneading and flattening the dough, run pieces of dough through until you have very flat, regular, rectangular pieces, beginning with a thick dough and gradually adjusting the dial for thinner and thinner pieces. Work slowly so that you don't rip the dough.

Use as it is, or cut into rectangles for cannelloni, lasagne or ravioli. Or put through the cutting side of the machine to form flat noodles, such as tagliatelle, according to the manufacturer's directions. Let the noodles dry as described on page 25 before stuffing or boiling.

COOKING METHODS

I will not be dogmatic about method: I prefer to give you several possible methods that I know work, and let you choose. In any case, noodles vary so much in the amount of time they need, depending on their freshness, their size, the amount of water and the size of the pot, that I think the only way of knowing when they are done is to taste constantly after the first 5 or 10 minutes (again, depending on size: the larger ones don't need tasting for at least 10 minutes).

Al dente means (and this is vague enough) the stage when the noodle is just firm enough to be firm and springy and not mushy to the tooth, but not so firm that it is hard at its core. You can only learn by trying; it is not a skill learned verbally.

When noodles reach this stage, drain them immediately in a colander and, unless otherwise specified, run cold water over them for a few seconds, tossing them a little. This rinses off starchiness that might make them sticky. It is a good idea to toss freshly cooked pasta with oil (olive, sesame, groundnut) or butter immediately after draining, depending on the recipe you are using.

Methods for Cooking Dry Pasta

Large Saucepan Boiling

Bring a 8–20-pint (4–10-litre) saucepan two-thirds full of water to a rolling boil. Add 1 tablespoon salt (some add the same of oil). Gradually add the noodles, so as not to stop the boiling, and stir once with a large fork, to separate the noodles. After the first 5 minutes for small or thin noodles, the first 10 minutes for thick ones, begin to taste. When *al dente*, drain quickly in a colander and rinse with cold water. Add oil or butter and toss.

Off-Heat Cooking Method for Macaroni and Thicker Noodles

Bring a large saucepan of water, as above, to a rolling boil and add the noodles all at once. Stir once. Put a tight-fitting lid on the pot,

turn the heat off completely, and don't open for 20 minutes. Drain well and proceed as above. (I prefer the first, since you can test the noodles more easily, but this is a good non-fuss method.)

Three-Step Chinese Method

Bring a large saucepan of water to a rolling boil and add the noodles. When they rise to the top, add ½ pint (250 ml) cold water. When it comes to the boil again, add another ½ pint (250 ml) cold water. When it boils the third time, the noodles should be done (taste). Drain the noodles and let them cool in a basin of cold water, if they are to be used in a cold recipe.

Method for Cooking Fresh Pasta

Bring a large saucepan of water to a rolling boil. Add 1 tablespoon salt, then the noodles, and cook for 3 to 5 minutes. Taste for doneness, then drain as above.

Double-cooked Noodles

1. Boil noodles *al dente* according to any method. Drain well and let dry slightly, spread on a large dish. Heat 2 tablespoons groundnut or olive oil in a wok or large frying pan. Fry the noodles, stirring, until browned.

2. Fry fresh or dry noodles in a heavy frying pan, with 2 tablespoons oil as above, *before* boiling. When browned, toss into a pot of boiling water and continue cooking, tasting after 3 minutes for fresh noodles, after 5 minutes for dried. Drain as above.

PURCHASING INGREDIENTS

Exotic Ingredients

Some of the ingredients in this book usually have to be bought from import grocers; each has been marked with an asterisk whenever it appears in a recipe.

The following can be bought at Middle Eastern or Indian grocery shops:

Chick-pea flour
Ground curry spices, including fenugreek seed
Kashmiri mirsch (a red pepper)
Mustard oil
Sesame paste (tahini)
Tamarind

The following can be bought in Chinese grocery shops:

Baby corn
Bamboo shoots
Barbecue sauce
Bean curd
Cabbage pickle
Chilli paste with garlic
Chinese cabbage
Chinese sausages
Crushed yellow beans
Dried bean curd skin
Dried lily flowers ('golden needles')
Dried mushrooms
Dried red chillies
Dried shrimp
Fishballs
Fish sauce
Fresh ginger
Hoisin sauce
Hot chilli oil
Noodles, fresh and dried (see pages 17–18)
Oyster sauce
Pea flour
Quail's eggs (tinned)
Rice flour
Salted, fermented black beans

Sesame oil
Szechuan preserved vegetable
Szechuan white peppercorns
Wood ear fungus

The following are specifically Japanese ingredients. Most of these can be bought from Chinese grocery shops, but some may need to be bought from Japanese shops, of which there are several in London.

Aonoriko (dried, pulverized seaweed)
Beni shoga (pickled ginger)
Daikon (long white horseradish) (can be bought in West Indian shops)
Dashi (Japanese soup stock)
Pickled vegetables
Rice wine vinegar
Sansho pepper
Togarashi (hot red pepper)

Wakame (dried seaweed)
Wasabi (horseradish) powder

The following can be bought from Italian grocery shops and delicatessens:

Chorizo	Mozzarella cheese
Clams (tinned)	Pine nuts
Dried Italian mushrooms	Ricotta cheese
Fontina cheese	Romano cheese
Fresh pasta	Romano pecorino cheese
Italian sausages, including peperoni	

GRATING CHEESES

For many of the dishes in this book, and not all of those Italian, the quality of the grating cheese is very important. It doesn't pay to buy

pregrated Parmesan or Romano in a shake-tin; they cost enough anyway, so you may as well spend a little more and get fresh hard cheeses to grate yourself. Buy a little hand cheese grater, or use an ordinary kitchen grater, and it is scarcely more work. And instead of always using Parmesan, try some of the others on this basic list of Italian grating cheeses.

Parmesan – the best of which is labelled *parmigiano reggiano*.
Romano – sharper, saltier than Parmesan. A sheep's milk cheese.
Romano pecorino – a variety of Romano, made from ewe's milk.
Caciocavallo – like an aged provolone.
Sardo – similar to Romano pecorino.

COOKING UTENSILS

The Wok

The wok, a frying pan that doubles as a saucepan, is an extremely important utensil in Chinese cooking. It is a simple round steel pan with a curved base. You will need a wok ring to hold it steady over the gas. (Although woks were originally intended for use with gas cookers, they can also be used on curly electric hotplates.)

You can cook food in many different ways in a wok, but most important of all you can stir-fry, a cross between frying and fast-boiling. Because of its high sides you can stir without things falling over the edge, as they would with a frying pan, and it doesn't get as steamy as a saucepan would.

The only snag with woks is that they need careful maintenance to keep them in good condition.

SOUPS

Mussel Noodle Soup

Mussels make an elegant first course for a large dinner. This soup is also excellent as a main course – perhaps thickened with a bit more spaghetti, and served with some fresh garlic bread.

8 tablespoons olive oil
2 cloves garlic, finely chopped
2 tablespoons tomato paste
Salt and freshly ground black pepper to taste
1 teaspoon oregano
1 tablespoon finely chopped fresh basil, or 1 teaspoon dried

2 pints (1 litre) water
3 dozen mussels in their shells, scrubbed well and beards scraped off
8 oz (250 g) spaghettini or ordinary spaghetti
1 bunch fresh parsley, chopped (about 8 tablespoons)

Heat the oil in a large saucepan. Add the garlic and brown lightly, then add the tomato paste, salt and pepper, oregano, basil, and the water. Bring to a simmer, then add the mussels. Cover and let simmer for about 10 minutes (when all the mussels are open, the soup will be done).

Meanwhile, boil the spaghettini or spaghetti *al dente* (see page 26). Drain well, place in a tureen, and pour the mussels and soup over. Serve, garnished with the parsley.

Fishball Soup

This is a very convenient sort of soup, since most of the ingredients can be in your larder if you live near a Chinese grocer. Fishballs are very delicate and unfishy and easily overwhelmed by stronger flavours – they are rather like delicate quenelles – so if you use the pungent, fresh coriander, use it lightly.

2½ pints (1¼ litres) chicken stock
Salt and pepper to taste
1½ tablespoons soy sauce
2 sheets dried bean curd skin,* soaked and shredded
5 dried mushrooms,* soaked and sliced, soaking water reserved
1 tin or packet Chinese fishballs (about 10),* drained

2 oz (60 g) vermicelli or Chinese bean thread noodles*
2 teaspoons sesame oil*
2 tablespoons chopped spring onions and fresh coriander or parsley

Put the stock on to heat and season with salt, pepper, and soy sauce. Add the bean curd skin and the mushrooms and their liquid, and bring to a simmer. Add the fishballs and vermicelli or Chinese bean thread noodles and simmer for 5 minutes.

Just before serving, add the sesame oil, spring onions, and coriander or parsley.

Clam Soup with Mushrooms and Small Shells

A more delicate concoction than traditional chowders, but reminiscent of the New England variety. A good main-dish soup, served with salad and crusty bread.

1½ tins (7 oz (220 g)) small clams*
1 medium onion, finely chopped
2 oz (60 g) butter
4 oz (125 g) fresh mushrooms, sliced
3 egg yolks
8 tablespoons milk

Salt and freshly ground black pepper to taste
1 tablespoon cornflour dissolved in 2 tablespoons warm water
½ pint (250 ml) chicken stock
2 oz (60 g) small shells
1 tablespoon chopped chives

Sauté the onion in 1 oz (30 g) of the butter until soft. Add the mushrooms and sauté over a high heat for a few minutes, then set aside.

Place the egg yolks in a soup tureen and beat them lightly with a fork while gradually adding the milk. Then add the remaining butter, which has been mashed until soft and creamy.

In a separate pot add ½ pint (250 ml) of water to the chicken stock and bring to the boil. Add the small shells and boil for a few minutes. Then slowly mix in the dissolved cornflour, and add the clams in their juices and the mushrooms.

Pour the hot soup very slowly into the egg yolk mixture, beating rapidly with a whisk as you pour, until all the soup has been added. Top with chopped chives and serve.

Hot and Sour Noodle Soup

Hot and sour soup must now be the most popular Chinese restaurant soup, pre-empting even wonton soup. This version with shrimp noodles is very rich and filling, and will certainly do as a main-course soup.

½ oz (15 g) dried lily flowers ('golden needles')*
½ oz (15 g) dried mushrooms*
½ oz (15 g) wood ear fungus*
3 tablespoons dried shrimp*
2½ pints (1¼ litres) chicken stock
2 tablespoons soy sauce
Salt and Tabasco to taste

2 oz (60 g) shrimp noodles* or thin egg vermicelli, broken up
1 teaspoon sesame oil*
Red wine vinegar to taste
1 tablespoon cornflour dissolved in 1 tablespoon cold water
2 eggs, beaten lightly
3 spring onions, shredded

Put the lily flowers, mushrooms, wood ear fungus, and shrimp into small, separate bowls. Cover with hot water and let soak for 20 minutes, then drain. Shred the lily flowers, mushrooms, and wood ear fungus.

Bring the stock to the boil in a heavy saucepan. Add the soaked ingredients, soy sauce, and salt and Tabasco to taste. Lower the heat, add the noodles, and simmer until the noodles are cooked.

Just before serving, stir in the sesame oil, vinegar to taste, the cornflour mixture, and the eggs, and stir for 1 minute while simmering. When thick, garnish with the spring onions and serve, along with extra vinegar and Tabasco.

Grandmother's Chicken Noodle Soup

This is the old favourite, but even more robust than the soup grandmother used to make. Now it can be the centrepiece of a dinner instead of just an appetizer. And the chicken that is left over will make a nice salad for another meal.

1 small chicken, left whole	1 bay leaf
3 stalks celery, including leaves, cleaned and chopped	6 peppercorns
1 medium onion, chopped	Salt and freshly ground pepper to taste
3 carrots, scraped and chopped	2 tablespoons finely chopped fresh parsley
4 sprigs fresh parsley	
1 large pinch dried thyme	4 oz (125 g) thin, flat egg noodles

Place the chicken in a large, heavy saucepan and add water to cover. Bring slowly to the boil, removing the scum as it floats to the top. When no more scum rises, let simmer and add the celery, onion, carrots, parsley, thyme, bay leaf, and peppercorns. Simmer gently, partially covered, for 2 or 3 hours, adding water as needed to keep the chicken covered.

Remove the chicken and set aside. Strain the soup well, discarding the soup vegetables. Pull the chicken meat from the bones and dice, reserving 8 oz (250 g) of the chicken for the soup and setting the rest aside for another meal.

Return the soup to the saucepan, along with salt and pepper to taste, the parsley, the chicken meat, and the noodles. Simmer until the noodles are tender, then serve.

Japanese Clear Chicken Soup with Vermicelli

It is said that a Japanese cook is judged by the clarity of his soup – it should be crystal clear and scarcely coloured. You should be able to gaze into the depths of the bowl and see the carefully arranged garnishes. Sometimes there may be a shred of black mushroom and a tiny pink shrimp, or a strip of lean pork and a crisp, bright green peapod. The garnishes provide aesthetic interest and contrasts in colour and texture. In this recipe, form the translucent noodles into a swirl suggesting a nest and add one sprig of cress and one strip of seaweed to the bits of chicken. Understatement is the key.

1 chicken breast (for a yield of 4oz (125 g) meat)
1¼ pints (625 ml) water
1¼ pints (625 ml) clear, rich chicken stock (or use tinned clear chicken soup)
1 teaspoon salt
Sansho pepper* to taste

3 oz (90 g) thin rice noodles or bean thread noodles,* soaked in warm water
6 small strips wakame (Japanese seaweed),* soaked in warm water
Watercress

Place the chicken breast, water, and stock in a saucepan and bring slowly to the boil. As the grey scum rises to the surface, carefully skim it off with a large spoon. When the stock begins to boil, immediately lower the heat to a bare simmer. Let simmer for 1 hour, partially covered, then strain well and set aside. Let the chicken breast cool.

When the chicken breast is cool, remove the skin and bones, then pull and cut the meat into neat shreds. Sprinkle them with salt and sansho pepper.

In separate serving bowls, place a swirl of noodles, chicken shreds, strips of wakame, and sprigs of watercress. Heat the soup just to a simmer and carefully pour over the ingredients arranged in the bowls.

Mandalay Coconut Khawksway

Lorna Chin of Boston's Mandalay Restaurant let me watch her in the kitchen making this and other wonderful Burmese dishes. The rich, hot, garlicky stock, smooth coconut milk, and crisp fried noodles make one of the best soups I've had. For a few weeks when we first discovered Mrs Chin, we had this dish at least once a week, at her place or ours.

8 tablespoons groundnut oil
2 large onions, finely chopped
8 cloves garlic, peeled and sliced
2 tablespoons very finely chopped fresh ginger*
2 fresh green chillies, seeded and finely chopped
2 dried red chillies,* mashed in a mortar
1 tablespoon ground turmeric*
2 teaspoons salt
1 oz (30 g) rice or pea flour*
1 tablespoon paprika

2½ pints (1¼ litres) water
3 lb (1½ kg) chicken pieces, cut up into small pieces, across the bones
1 lb (500 g) thin egg noodles
1¼ pints (625 ml) Coconut 'Milk' (see below)
1 bunch spring onions, chopped (about 8 tablespoons)
Crunchy fried noodles (shop-bought, or see note below)
Lemon wedges

Heat the oil in a heavy saucepan. Add the onion, garlic, and ginger and sauté until lightly browned. Add the fresh chillies, then lower the heat and let simmer into a paste, stirring occasionally. It will take 4 or 5 minutes.

Add the dried chillies, turmeric, salt, rice or pea flour, and paprika and stir-fry for 3 minutes over a medium heat. Add the water and bring to the boil; then lower the heat to a simmer. Add the chicken pieces, cover, and let simmer for 40 minutes.

Remove the chicken pieces and set aside. Continue to simmer the soup, uncovered, for 2 to 3 hours.

Boil the egg noodles in salted water *al dente* (see page 26), then drain and place in a serving dish. Taste the soup for seasoning, then add the coconut 'milk' and heat to a simmer. Add the chicken pieces, heat through, and pour both chicken and soup over the noodles. Garnish with the spring onions, fried noodles, and lemon wedges.

Note: Instead of buying fried noodles, you can cut up cooked spaghetti and deep-fry it until golden. Drain well before you use it.

Coconut 'Milk'

Let 6 oz (190 g) unsweetened coconut shreds, or grated fresh coconut, sit in 1¼ pints (625 ml) hot water for 1 hour. Pour into a clean cloth held over a bowl and squeeze the liquid through the cloth.

Pour the liquid through the coconut again, and you will have 1¼ pints (625 ml) of 'milk'.

Ham and Bean Thread Soup

This soup is an original combination of appealing Asian tastes. But don't hesitate to serve it as the first course of a Western meal. One caution: be sure to separate the bean threads as you place them in the soup. Once I didn't and had a very hard time getting them apart before serving the soup.

1 bag dashi* (Japanese soup stock)
1½ pints (750 ml) boiling water
5 dried mushrooms,* soaked in warm water for 20 minutes, soaking water reserved
3 thick slices smoked ham

1 tablespoon soy sauce
1 teaspoon sesame oil*
Salt to taste
2 oz (60 g) bean thread noodles*
2 spring onions, chopped

Place the dashi bag in the boiling water and simmer for 20 minutes.

Squeeze the mushrooms dry, then slice and add to the soup, along with the water they soaked in. Cut the ham into shreds and add to the simmering soup, along with the soy sauce, sesame oil, and salt to taste.

Boil the bean thread in 2 pints (1 litre) water until soft – about 5 minutes – then drain, separating the noodles as you add them to the soup. Add the chopped spring onions just before serving.

Vietnamese Pho (Beef Soup)

Pho is a very popular Vietnamese soup that is often a main dish. The amount of fish sauce can be adjusted. It is a peculiar taste at first, and needs some getting used to. If you can't find it, try using half the quantity of anchovy paste.

2 lb (1 kg) beef shin
3 medium onions, finely chopped
2 tablespoons very finely chopped
    ginger*
¼ teaspoon ground fennel seeds
1 teaspoon salt
4 oz (125 g) vermicelli (Italian) or
    Homemade Noodles (see below)

1 tablespoon vinegar
2 tablespoons fish sauce*
Chopped spring onions and
    shredded fresh green chillies
    for garnish

Place the beef in a 6-pint (3-litre) saucepan and cover with water. Bring to the boil, skimming, then reduce the heat and simmer for 3 hours, or until tender. Remove the beef and cool.

Meanwhile, add the onions, ginger, fennel seeds, and salt to the stock and simmer for 15 minutes. Add the vermicelli or fresh noodles and simmer for 8 minutes longer, then add the vinegar, the fish sauce, and the meat, removed from the bones and shredded. Garnish with the spring onions and chillies and serve.

Homemade Noodles

4 oz (125 g) plain flour
1 egg
4 tablespoons water

Combine all the ingredients and knead until smooth. Force the dough through a potato ricer, colander or large-holed sieve, into the boiling soup.

Soupe à la Ahmed

A fairly unusual noodle-vegetable soup, quite sufficient for a supper with crusty bread and salad. This North African mixture reminds me a bit of Ukrainian bortsch and a little of minestrone. The lemon at the end is quite essential.

4 oz (125 g) margarine or 8 tablespoons olive oil

3 medium onions, sliced thin

3 cloves garlic, very finely chopped

3 large carrots, scraped and sliced

1 large potato, peeled and diced

⅓ head red cabbage, thinly sliced

1 large tin (28 oz (875 g) size)
Italian plum tomatoes, plus 1
small tin (8 oz (250 g) size)

½ tin (5 oz (160 g)) tomato paste

3 stalks celery, diced

2 small courgettes, diced

8 oz (250 g) lean boneless lamb,
shredded

½ teaspoon each dried rosemary,
thyme, basil, and cayenne
pepper

5 pints (2½ litres) water

3 or 4 swirls of thin egg noodles

3 oz (90 g) orzo (rice-shaped
pasta)

3 tablespoons chopped fresh
parsley

Lemon wedges

Heat the oil or margarine in a very large, heavy saucepan, then add the onions and garlic and sauté until golden. Add all the other ingredients except the egg noodles, orzo, parsley, and lemon wedges. Bring to the boil, then reduce the heat and simmer for 45 minutes.

Add the egg noodles and orzo and cook for 10 minutes longer, then serve, garnished with the parsley and accompanied by lemon wedges.

Passatelli in Brodo

This soup could scarcely be simpler. A greatly comforting dish, a midnight snack, a prelude to a heavier meal, a convalescent treat. These *passatelli* are halfway between a dumpling and a noodle – a little firmer than the Roman *stracciatella*, which is closer to an egg-drop soup, and less firm than spaetzle.

2½ pints (1¼ litres) beef or chicken
stock

Salt and freshly ground pepper to
taste

1 bay leaf

½ teaspoon thyme

5 eggs

5 tablespoons freshly grated Parmesan cheese

5 tablespoons dry breadcrumbs

White pepper

Put the stock into a large saucepan. Season with the salt, pepper, bay leaf, and thyme, then bring to the boil.

Meanwhile, combine the eggs, Parmesan, breadcrumbs, and salt and white pepper to taste in a small saucepan. Heat, stirring to blend, only a minute or so, then, holding a potato ricer, colander or large-holed sieve over the broth, which should now be boiling, press the paste into the soup. Let simmer a few minutes, then serve with more grated Parmesan.

Pasta in Brodo with Stracciatella

Like *passatelli*, this soup is a comfort. The tiny 'peppercorn' pasta provides interesting texture and contrast to the wisps of cheesy egg-drop. *Stracciatella* is one of the most common Roman preludes to a meal.

5 tablespoons acini di pepe ('peppercorn' soup pasta)	3 tablespoons freshly grated Parmesan cheese
2½ pints (1¼ litres) chicken stock	Salt and freshly ground black pepper to taste
3 eggs	

Boil the acini di pepe for 6 minutes then drain.

Heat the chicken stock in a saucepan. While it is getting hot, combine the eggs and Parmesan in a mixing bowl, beating with a fork. Add the noodles to the soup, and simmer gently for 1 minute, then, using a fork, stir the soup rapidly in a circular motion to set up a whirlpool. Dribble the egg mixture in, as the soup swirls around, to form shreds; in a minute or so, the egg will set. Serve immediately, with salt and pepper to taste.

Hungarian Vegetable Soup with 'Pinched Noodles'

This is like a minestrone, but with dumpling-like noodles floating in it, with sour cream and dill, it is a hearty main-dish soup.

8 oz (250 g) small white beans
2½ oz (75 g) butter
2 stalks celery, finely chopped
1 carrot, peeled and finely chopped
1 large onion, finely chopped

2 large tomatoes, chopped
1 oz (30 g) plain flour
½ pint (250 ml) sour cream
2 tablespoons dill, finely chopped
Hungarian csipetke (see page 220)

Soak beans in cold water overnight. Drain and place in a saucepan. Add 2½ pints (1¼ litres) water and bring to the boil. Simmer 1 hour or more, until beans are done (it depends on the age of the beans).

In a heavy saucepan, melt 1 oz (30 g) of the butter, and sauté the celery, carrot and onion until golden and soft. Add to beans in their liquid, together with the tomato, and simmer ½ hour.

Melt the rest of the butter in a saucepan and stir in the flour. Cook, stirring, for 3 minutes. Add ½ pint (250 ml) of stock from the beans, stirring to combine. Cook until thick, then pour the mixture into the soup and bring just to the boil. Reduce heat. Slowly stir in sour cream, then add noodle dough and cook until the noodles rise to the surface. Serve garnished with dill.

Broccoli Soup with Spinach Noodles

This is a new twist on a favourite Roman soup, which blends the flavours of ham and broccoli. The spinach noodles make it doubly green. Be sure to drain off most of the salt pork fat or the soup will be too greasy for most palates.

2 tablespoons olive oil
2 cloves garlic, very finely chopped
2 onions, very finely chopped
4 slices ham, diced
Freshly ground black pepper to taste
1 lb (500 g) broccoli, separated into florets

4 oz (125 g) salt pork, diced
1 oz (30 g) butter
1¼ pints (625 ml) chicken stock
3–4 oz (90–125 g) green spinach noodles, broken into small pieces
1 oz (30 g) Parmesan cheese, freshly grated

Heat the olive oil in a large pot, then sauté the garlic, onion, and ham until soft. Add the pepper and enough water to cover and simmer, covered, for about 20 minutes.

In another pot, cover the broccoli florets with water and cook until tender but still crisp.

In a saucepan sauté the salt pork in the butter until crisp, then drain off most of the fat. Place the drained broccoli in the pan with the salt pork and simmer for 5 minutes, then add to the ham mixture, making sure it is well blended. Stir in the chicken stock and bring to a simmer.

Meanwhile, cook the pasta *al dente* (see page 26). Drain and add to the soup, then serve, topping each portion with the Parmesan cheese.

Minestrone Milanese

This is a delicious variation on a classic Italian soup. Take special care in cooking the vegetables added at the end. If they retain some of their crisp texture, the soup is fresher tasting.

3 medium onions, finely chopped
3 carrots, scraped and finely chopped
2 parsnips, scraped and finely chopped
3 cloves garlic, finely chopped
3 chicken or beef bouillon cubes
1½ oz (45 g) butter or 3 tablespoons oil
Salt and freshly ground black pepper to taste
1 bay leaf
1½ pints (750 ml) water

1 large tin (28 oz (875 g) size) Italian plum tomatoes, plus 1 small tin (8 oz (250 g) size), drained and roughly chopped
3 oz (90 g) white beans, cooked, or half a 14 oz (440 g) tin
3 medium courgettes, sliced
3 oz (90 g) pastina or orzo (rice-shaped pasta)
2 oz (60 g) fresh (shelled) or frozen peas
2 tablespoons chopped fresh parsley

In a large, heavy saucepan, sauté the onion, carrots, parsnips, and garlic in the butter or oil until tender. Add the bouillon, salt, pepper bay leaf, and water. Bring to the boil, then reduce the heat and simmer for 30 minutes. Add the tomatoes and simmer for 30 minutes longer. (The soup can be set aside at this point.)

Half an hour before serving, add the beans and courgettes and bring to a simmer. Add the noodles and peas and cook just until the noodles are tender. Serve garnished with parsley, and pass round crusty garlic bread and freshly grated Romano cheese.

Summer Minestrone

Minestrone is certainly not a hot weather soup, which is a shame, since summer is when all the vegetables are at their best. Though most of the traditional ingredients are missing, this version still leaves you with a refreshing summer shadow of the heavier minestrones.

1 tablespoon olive oil
1 small onion, finely chopped
2 cloves garlic, finely chopped
4 medium tomatoes, peeled, seeded, and finely chopped (see note below)
2 pints (1 litre) chicken stock
1 oz (30 g) vermicelli, broken into small bits

2 small courgettes, thinly sliced
1 green pepper, finely chopped
Salt and freshly ground black pepper to taste
2 tablespoons chopped fresh parsley

Heat the olive oil in a large, heavy saucepan. Add the onion and sauté until golden, then add the garlic and stir for 1 minute. Add the tomatoes and chicken stock and bring to the boil. Cook for 15 minutes, then add the vermicelli and courgettes and cook for 5 minutes, or until the vermicelli is tender. Add the green pepper and remove from the heat. Chill.

To serve, add salt and freshly ground black pepper to taste and garnish with parsley.

Note: Peel the tomatoes by putting them into boiling water for 20 seconds or so and draining; the skin should peel off easily. Cut in half and squeeze gently over sink or bowl in order to remove the seeds.

Mexican Vermicelli Soup

One unusual aspect of this recipe is the sautéing of the noodles before they are cooked in the soup, which gives them a pleasant, nutty taste; the method can be tried in other noodle recipes. This is quite a straightforward soup, which gains in sophistication when the sherry is added.

2 tablespoons olive oil
2 oz (60 g) vermicelli or fine egg noodles
1 onion, chopped
1 clove garlic, finely chopped
4 medium tomatoes, peeled, seeded, and chopped (see note above)

3 pints (1½ litres) beef stock (not bouillon)
Salt and freshly ground black pepper to taste
Pinch of granulated sugar
1 tablespoon chopped fresh parsley
4 tablespoons dry sherry

Heat the oil in a heavy saucepan. Sauté the uncooked noodles until golden brown, then drain and set aside.

Put the onion, garlic, and tomato in the blender and blend until uniform but not liquefied. Cook this mixture in the oil remaining in the pan for 5 minutes, stirring constantly. Add the noodles, stock, and seasoning, then cover and simmer until the noodles are tender.

Add the parsley and sherry and serve, offering freshly grated Parmesan cheese separately.

EGGS AND CHEESE

Broad Noodles and Three Cheeses

Strong Cheddar is important in this robust dish, a very simple variant of macaroni cheese.

1 8 oz (250 g) tin Italian plum tomatoes, blended until smooth, mixed with 2 tablespoons tomato paste
Salt and freshly ground black pepper
2 teaspoons chopped fresh basil or 1 teaspoon dried

1 lb (500 g) broad egg noodles
8 oz (250 g) strong Cheddar cheese, finely crumbled
4 oz (125 g) cottage cheese
2 oz (60 g) Romano pecorino,* freshly grated

Preheat the oven to 350°F (175°C), mark 4.

Season the tomato purée with salt, pepper, and the basil, then pour into a greased casserole.

Boil the noodles *al dente* (see page 26), then toss with the Cheddar and season with salt and pepper. Put in the casserole and top with the cottage cheese, well crumbled, and the Romano pecorino. Bake for 30 minutes, or until lightly browned.

Macaronatha

Feta gives noodles a sharp and memorable flavour. Once you have added the butter, the faster you can serve this dish the better it will taste. You should be eating it just as the feta softens, and before the noodles have settled into a mass.

1 lb (500 g) fresh noodles (see   4 oz (125 g) unsalted butter
  pages 22–3)
4 or 5 oz (125–160 g) feta cheese,*
  crumbled

Boil the noodles *al dente* (see page 26), then drain well and place in a serving bowl. Sprinkle the cheese over the noodles and mix well.

Melt the butter in a heavy saucepan, and when it is just beginning to brown, pour it quickly over the noodles. Toss lightly and serve at once.

Spaghetti with Kephalotiri Cheese and Browned Butter

Kephalotiri is a difficult cheese to find if you don't live in an area that has Greek grocers. Search a little. Although I haven't tried it myself, I hear that it freezes well, so if you do find some, get extra and put it aside for the future.

Browned butter with noodles is quite delicious, as are slightly burned noodles; you could also sauté the cooked noodles in butter until both are browned.

1 lb (500 g) spaghettini or   Salt and freshly ground black
  ordinary spaghetti   pepper to taste
2½ oz (75 g) butter
8 oz (250 g) kephalotiri cheese,
  crumbled

Boil the spaghettini or spaghetti *al dente* (see page 26). Drain well, then put in a serving bowl.

Heat the butter carefully in a heavy frying pan. Let it get to a deep brown, but don't let it burn. Toss the pasta with the kephalotiri and brown butter and add salt and plenty of pepper. Serve at once.

German Kummelkase Noodle Mould

Caraway cheese makes an unusual macaroni cheese. Use this mould as a case for buttered broccoli or garlic prawns.

8 oz (250 g) egg noodles, boiled *al dente* and drained
8 fl oz (200 ml) milk, scalded (heated to just below boiling point)
3 eggs, beaten

4 oz (125 g) caraway cheese, grated (kummelkase: use German, or any of the various Scandinavian varieties)
1 teaspoon salt
Pinch of cayenne pepper

Preheat oven to 325°F (160°C), mark 3.

Beat eggs in a mixing bowl. Slowly pour hot milk into the eggs, whisking continually. Add cheese, salt and pepper. Combine this with the noodles, and pour into a buttered ring mould. Bake until firm, about 45 minutes. Unmould.

Macaroni Cheese

Macaroni cheese is an old standby, but it is surprising how much a little attention to detail can improve what would ordinarily be just another meal. For instance, buttering the casserole well and coating with breadcrumbs produces the crust people fight over.

8 oz (250 g) elbow macaroni
1 oz (30 g) butter
1 oz (30 g) plain flour
¾ pint (375 ml) milk, scalded (heated to just below boiling point)
6 oz (190 g) medium strong Cheddar cheese, roughly grated

1 teaspoon salt
Freshly ground black pepper to taste
Dash each of Tabasco and Worcestershire sauce
1 oz (30 g) breadcrumbs
1 oz (30 g) Parmesan cheese, freshly grated

Preheat the oven to 325°F (160°C), mark 3.

Boil the macaroni *al dente* to a *firm* stage (see page 26).

Meanwhile, heat the butter in a saucepan. Stir in the flour and let bubble for 1 minute, then add the milk, whisking as you do so to prevent lumps. Let simmer as the mixture thickens, then stir in the Cheddar until it is melted. Add, off the heat, the salt, pepper, Tabasco, and Worcestershire sauce.

Combine the breadcrumbs and Parmesan cheese. Butter a small casserole well and coat with 4 tablespoons of the breadcrumb mixture. Drain the macaroni and toss with the sauce. Pour into the casserole, top with the remaining breadcrumb mixture, and bake in the preheated oven for 45 minutes to 1 hour, until crusty brown.

Noodles with Cottage Cheese and Peas

This is lighter and fresher tasting than many other cheesy noodle dishes, for the noodles are tossed with the cheese instead of being baked into it. Do not neglect to add sugar and something crisp and green – peas, as suggested below, or perhaps finely shredded green peppers, or strips of fresh fennel.

1½ lb (750 g) egg noodles	only 4 or 5 minutes, until *just*
1 oz (30 g) butter or margarine	tender, or another green vege-
8 oz (250 g) cottage cheese	table
1 bunch spring onions, chopped	1 teaspoon granulated sugar
(about 8 tablespoons)	Salt and freshly ground black
2 oz (60 g) shelled peas, cooked	pepper to taste

Boil the noodles *al dente* (see page 26). Drain and place in a bowl; add the butter or margarine and toss well. Add the cheese, tossing with a fork, then toss with the spring onions and the peas or other vegetable. Season to taste with the sugar, salt, and pepper and serve immediately.

Spaghetti Tossed with Cheese

What a simple dish! Yet the mingling of different cheeses produces a subtle flavour often lacking in more complicated recipes. Naturally, you may want to experiment with your own combination of cheeses.

1½ lb (750 g) spaghetti

2 oz (60 g) Gruyère cheese, freshly grated

2 oz (60 g) Parmesan cheese, freshly grated

2 oz (60 g) Fontina cheese,* freshly grated

4 oz (125 g) butter, melted

Salt and freshly ground black pepper to taste

Cook the spaghetti *al dente* (see page 26), then drain well and place in a large warmed bowl. Toss with the cheeses, pouring the hot butter over all. Toss again, adding salt and pepper, and serve at once.

Spaghetti with Yogurt Sauce

A recipe that shows just how quickly it is possible to assemble a pasta dish that is both interesting in flavour and inexpensive. For a heavier dish, you can substitute ricotta for the yogurt.

1 lb (500 g) spaghetti
½ oz (15 g) butter
2 tablespoons olive oil
1 small onion, finely chopped
3 cloves garlic, finely chopped

3 tablespoons tomato paste
Salt and freshly ground black
   pepper to taste
½ pint (250 ml) natural yogurt

Cook the spaghetti *al dente* (see page 26), then drain and toss with the butter. Set aside and keep warm.

Heat the oil in a heavy frying pan. Add the onion and garlic and sauté until golden, then stir in the tomato paste. Season with salt and pepper.

Turn off the heat and stir in the yogurt. Toss with the spaghetti and serve.

Noodles Romanoff

This is an especially rich combination of noodles, sour cream, and cheese that will satisfy a large crowd of people. It can be frozen for weeks, or refrigerated a few days before baking. Very suitable for a buffet supper.

1 lb (500 g) fine noodles
1 lb (500 g) cream cheese,
   softened
1 pint (½ litre) sour cream
1 small onion, very finely chopped
1 teaspoon Worcestershire sauce

½ teaspoon garlic salt
Dash of Tabasco
1 teaspoon salt
1 oz (30 g) buttered breadcrumbs
   (see note below)

Preheat the oven to 350°F (175°C), mark 4.

Cook the noodles *al dente* (see page 26), then drain and place in a large bowl.

Combine the cream cheese, sour cream, onion, and seasonings, stirring well to mix, then stir into the cooked noodles. Pour into a greased 4-pint (2-litre) casserole, top with the breadcrumbs, and bake for about 25 minutes.

Note: For buttered breadcrumbs, melt ½ oz (15 g) butter for every 2 oz (60 g) breadcrumbs and stir until well mixed.

Omelette aux Nouilles

Omelettes can be vehicles for many leftovers, and noodles work well in this one. Beside mushrooms, you might also add chopped vegetables – spinach, green beans, broccoli – almost anything will do.

2 tablespoons herbs (fresh chives, parsley, thyme, tarragon, in whatever mixture you like)
8 eggs
1 teaspoon salt
Freshly ground black pepper to taste

3 oz (90 g) thin noodles, cooked
1½ oz (45 g) butter
2 oz (60 g) mushrooms, sliced and sautéed in 1 oz (30 g) butter

Combine the fresh herbs, eggs, salt, pepper, and noodles.

Heat the butter in a large frying pan until bubbly, then pour in the egg-noodle mixture and cook, without stirring, over a medium heat until the edges and bottom are set. Sprinkle the mushrooms over the top, then, using a spatula, fold one side over the other. Remove from the pan and serve.

Note: If you prefer to serve the omelette unfolded, cover it and let cook until set.

Cheese Noodle Soufflé

A soufflé seems an odd place to find a noodle, yet the contrast is delicious. The dish is like an aerated, delicate macaroni cheese.

8 oz (250 g) macaroni or noodles, cooked *al dente*, and drained well
5 eggs, separated
Generous ½ pint (250 ml) White Sauce (page 227)
Salt and freshly ground black pepper to taste

Freshly grated nutmeg to taste
3 oz (90 g) Gruyère cheese, freshly grated
1 oz (30 g) Parmesan cheese, freshly grated

Preheat the oven to 400°F (200°C), mark 6.

Cook the noodles *al dente* (see page 26), then drain well and place in a well buttered casserole.

Add the egg yolks, one by one, to the white sauce, beating well. Season with salt, pepper, and nutmeg and stir in the Gruyère. Fold in the egg whites, stiffly beaten.

Top the noodles with the egg mixture, sprinkle with the Parmesan, and bake in the preheated oven for 45 minutes, or until puffed and brown.

Macaroni Georgina

A nice, quick luncheon dish. The eggs should be soft boiled, and shelled carefully. The centres should run when cut into.

6 eggs
1 lb (500 g) small macaroni
2 cloves garlic, very finely chopped
1½ oz (45 g) butter, softened
8 oz (250 g) fresh mushrooms, sliced and sautéed in 1 oz (30 g) butter until soft
Salt and freshly ground black pepper to taste

Boil the eggs for 5 minutes, or long enough to set the whites but leave the yolks soft. Shell them carefully and set aside, covered to keep warm.

Boil the macaroni *al dente* (see page 26), then drain. Sauté the garlic in butter until golden. Toss the macaroni in the garlic butter, then add the mushrooms and salt and pepper and toss lightly.

Serve with the eggs in the centre of a 'nest' of noodles.

Cottage Cheese and Sour Cream Noodle Pudding

This is a relative of the great family of Jewish noodle puddings, which are usually sweet.

1½ lb (750 g) curly egg noodles
4 oz (125 g) butter or margarine
½ pint (250 ml) sour cream
12 oz (375 g) cottage cheese
2 eggs
3 spring onions, finely chopped

½ teaspoon dillweed or 2 tablespoons finely chopped fresh
dill
Salt and freshly ground black
pepper to taste

Preheat the oven to 350°F (175°C), mark 4.

Boil the noodles for 5 minutes, then drain and toss first with the butter, then with the remaining ingredients. Place in a buttered casserole and bake for 1 hour, or until browned.

Cannelloni with Spinach and Feta Filling

Well worth the effort. Homemade pasta squares for this dish make all the difference, but the filling can be used in bought cannelloni or shells, boiled *al dente* (see page 26) before stuffing. In either case, you can assemble the whole thing ahead of time, to be frozen or refrigerated before baking.

8 oz (250 g) spinach, washed and
  picked over
2 onions, finely chopped
2 cloves garlic, finely chopped
1 oz (30 g) butter
4 oz (125 g) feta cheese, crumbled
4 oz (125 g) cottage cheese
Pinch of freshly grated nutmeg

Salt and freshly ground black
  pepper to taste
2 eggs
4 tablespoons chopped fresh
  parsley
Fresh Egg Pasta (page 23)
1¼ pints (625 ml) Fresh Tomato
  Sauce (page 225)

Sauté the onion and garlic in the butter in a deep saucepan until golden. Remove from the heat and stir in the spinach and the two cheeses. Beat in the seasonings, eggs, and parsley, then refrigerate while you prepare the pasta dough.

Roll the dough out as thin as possible and cut it into 3 × 5-inch (7 × 12-cm) rectangles. Let these dry on clean cloths for at least 1 hour, then cook them for 3 to 5 minutes in a large saucepan of boiling, salted water. Drain and place on cloths.

Butter a 9 × 13 × 2-inch (22 × 32 × 5-cm) baking dish. Place about 2 tablespoons of the filling on each rectangle and roll up. Place side by side, seam side down, in the baking dish. Pour tomato sauce over all. (At this point, you may refrigerate or freeze.)

Preheat the oven to 350°F (175°C), mark 4. Bake the cannelloni for 30 minutes, or until bubbly. Serve immediately, offering freshly grated Parmesan cheese separately.

Macaroni Cheese with Spinach

Here is another pleasant change from the usual macaroni cheese. You might try other parboiled or sautéed vegetables, like aubergine or Swiss chard.

2 oz (60 g) butter
1 oz (30 g) plain flour
¾ pint (375 ml) milk
1 teaspoon salt
Freshly ground black pepper and
  nutmeg to taste

8 oz (250 g) spinach, washed and
  picked over
8 oz (250 g) strong Cheddar
  cheese, grated
4 oz (125 g) macaroni, cooked
4 tablespoons breadcrumbs

Preheat the oven to 350°F (175°C), mark 4.

Heat the butter in a saucepan until it melts. Add the flour and whisk, then add the milk gradually, while beating, and bring to a simmer, stirring as the sauce thickens. Add the salt, pepper, and nutmeg and simmer for 3 minutes.

Meanwhile, cook the spinach in the water remaining on the leaves until wilted, then drain well.

Stir all but 2 tablespoons of the cheese into the sauce and remove from the heat. In a buttered baking dish, layer the macaroni, spinach, and cheese sauce. Sprinkle with the breadcrumbs and remaining 2 tablespoons of cheese and bake for 45 minutes, or until bubbly and browned.

Turos Csusza

A baked Hungarian noodle casserole, which can be assembled in 20 minutes, and baked in another 30. Among many virtues, it can be prepared well in advance and baked just before serving.

6 rashers bacon, cooked until crisp and crumbled

12 oz (375 g) wide egg noodles, cooked *al dente* (about 7 minutes), drained and tossed with 2 tablespoons of the bacon fat

½ pint (250 ml) sour cream at room temperature

8 oz (250 g) cottage cheese

3 tablespoons chopped spring onions

Salt and freshly ground black pepper to taste

Preheat oven to 350°F (175°C), mark 4.

Mix noodles, sour cream, cottage cheese, half the bacon, spring onions and salt and pepper. Pour into buttered casserole, sprinkle with remaining bacon, and bake for 30 minutes, until bubbly and brown.

Odamaki-mushi
(Japanese Noodle Custard)

A variant on *chawan-mushi*, a savoury custard, *odamaki-mushi* includes noodles and other bits hidden in the steamed egg base. You could use prawns instead of chicken, and you may add tinned gingko nuts, small cubes of bean curd, fresh mangetouts, or a few fresh or frozen green peas to each cup.

1 whole chicken breast, raw, boned and cut into ½-inch (1-cm) cubes

2 oz (60 g) bean thread noodles,* soaked in warm water for 15 minutes and drained

Peas, mangetouts, bean curd,* chopped spring onion or whatever contrasting taste texture elements you choose

1 teaspoon soy sauce

Salt and sansho pepper* to taste

6 medium eggs

1 pint (500 ml) stock or dashi*

Beni shoga (pickled ginger)* for garnish

In each of 6 small custard cups or heatproof bowls, place a few cubes of chicken and a small swirl of noodles. Add a bit of whatever other ingredients you choose, then sprinkle with ½ teaspoon of the soy sauce, salt, and sansho pepper and set aside.

In a mixing bowl, beat the eggs well. Add the stock or dashi, ½ teaspoon salt, and ½ teaspoon soy sauce, then divide the mixture between the cups. Cover each cup with foil.

If you have a large steamer, use it. If not, place a rack (a preserving rack will do) or upside-down plate in a large saucepan. Place the cups on the rack and add boiling water carefully up to the bottom of the cups, but not touching them. Cover the pot and steam over a moderate heat for 10 to 15 minutes, or until the custard is firm. Serve lukewarm, garnished with the pickled ginger.

VEGETABLES

VEGETABLES

Pesto Genovese

Pesto is a real treat, even more so because to make it I have to denude half my crop of carefully tended basil – but it is worth it. Some who love it are tempted to make it in the basil-less winter by using dried basil in combination with parsley. Don't. Use freshly grated Romano and pine nuts, if you can find them. Covered tightly, it keeps for a week to ten days in the refrigerator, and can be used on cold prawns or boiled chicken as well.

8 tablespoons (about ½ oz (15 g)) chopped fresh parsley
8 tablespoons chopped fresh basil leaves
4 cloves garlic, chopped
3 oz (90 g) pine nuts*
2 oz (60 g) Romano cheese, freshly grated
Salt and freshly ground black pepper to taste
Italian olive oil as needed (approximately ½ pint (250 ml))
2 lb (1 kg) spaghetti

Place the parsley and basil in the container of a blender, about half at a time of each. To each batch add half the garlic, pine nuts and cheese, and salt and pepper to taste, and then add the olive oil gradually, blending until smooth.

Boil the spaghetti *al dente* (see page 26). Drain and toss with the pesto sauce, then serve, offering extra freshly grated Romano separately.

Roman Spaghetti

Tossing the cooked spaghetti in a flavoured oil until browned before adding the tomato sauce gives this dish a certain depth of character. Using a Chinese wok and stir-frying helps to brown it quickly.

1½ lb (750 g) spaghetti
8 tablespoons olive oil
2 medium onions, chopped
1 clove garlic, very finely chopped

1 tablespoon fresh basil or 1½ teaspoons dried
1¼ pints (625 ml) Fresh Tomato Sauce (see page 225)

Boil the spaghetti *al dente* (see page 26), then drain very well.

Heat the oil in a heavy frying pan or wok. Add the onion and garlic and sauté until golden, then add the basil. Add the spaghetti and toss over a high heat until well mixed, browned, and heated through, then toss with the tomato sauce.

Serve immediately, offering freshly grated Romano cheese separately.

Broccoli and Anchovy Sauce
with Small Shells

Broccoli and anchovies, both strong tastes, do not war with each other in this combination. Keep the broccoli *al dente* – undercooked – for preference. When it is overdone, its colour changes to a sort of army olive and it has a sickly taste and texture.

1 medium head broccoli, cut into small florets
2 tablespoons olive oil
1 tin (2 oz (60 g)) anchovy fillets, chopped
1½ oz (45 g) butter

Salt and freshly ground black pepper to taste
8 oz (250 g) small macaroni shells
1½ oz (45 g) Parmesan or Romano* cheese, freshly grated

Cook the broccoli in boiling water until just tender, about 5 minutes then drain and set aside.

Place the oil in a frying pan over a medium heat and add the chopped anchovies. Mash the anchovies into a paste with a wooden spoon, then sauté the broccoli in the anchovy sauce for about 5 minutes, adding 1 oz (30 g) of the butter to thicken the sauce. Add salt and pepper to taste.

Meanwhile, boil the shells *al dente* (see page 26), drain them, and mix with the remaining butter and the grated cheese. Then pour the broccoli and anchovy sauce over the shells and serve.

Tagliatelle alla Romana

A classic combination of peas, ham, and freshly made pasta. The trick is to have everything done at once, and to toss it all together just before eating. One often sees this dish assembled in a chafing dish at table.

1 lb (500 g) fresh tagliatelle, home-made (see pages 22–3) or shop-bought*

3 oz (90 g) butter, softened

4 oz (125 g) Romano cheese,* freshly grated

8 tablespoons double cream, heated (*not* boiled)

1 lb (500 g) fresh peas, shelled and parboiled (or use 6 oz (180 g) frozen)

4 oz (125 g) ham, finely shredded

Salt and freshly ground black pepper to taste

Boil the tagliatelle *al dente* (see page 26). Place the butter in a serving dish, then drain the tagliatelle in a colander and add to the butter. Add the cheese, cream, peas, and ham and toss well. Serve immediately with salt and pepper to taste.

Mixed Vegetables with Pasta

A variant on the mixed vegetable sauce, this time with bacon and a little wine. Very hearty.

4 rashers bacon
4 tablespoons olive oil
1 bunch fresh parsley, chopped (about 8 tablespoons)
6 spring onions, chopped
2 cloves garlic, very finely chopped
1 medium red onion, very finely chopped
2 tablespoons chopped fresh basil or 1 tablespoon dried
½ small head cabbage, shredded
8 oz (250 g) courgettes, scrubbed and diced

8 oz (250 g) tomatoes, peeled, seeded, and chopped (see note on page 49)
2 green peppers, seeded and diced
½ pint (250 ml) chicken stock
1 tablespoon dry vermouth
Salt and freshly ground pepper to taste
1 lb (500 g) fresh tagliatelle, homemade (see pages 22–3) or shopbought,* or spaghetti
1 oz (30 g) butter
Freshly grated Parmesan cheese

In a large, heavy saucepan, sauté the bacon until crisp. Add the oil, parsley, spring onions, garlic, and onion and sauté for 3 minutes, then add the basil, cabbage, courgettes, tomatoes, green peppers, chicken stock, vermouth, and salt and pepper to taste. Simmer, uncovered, for 10 minutes.

Cook the pasta *al dente* (see page 26), then drain and toss first with the butter, then with the vegetable mixture. Serve immediately, offering freshly grated Parmesan cheese separately.

Penne all'Arrabiata

'Angry penne' is the translation of the above. 'Angry' with hot red chillies, I suppose. This is very delicious and fiery dish.

1 oz (30 g) butter
2 cloves garlic, finely chopped
5 tomatoes, peeled, seeded, and chopped (see note on page 49)
3 fresh red hot chilli peppers, seeded and finely chopped
1 tablespoon finely chopped fresh basil or 1½ teaspoons dried

Salt and freshly ground black pepper to taste
1 lb (500 g) penne ('quill' noodles)
1 oz (30 g) Romano pecorino cheese,* freshly grated
1 oz (30 g) Parmesan cheese, freshly grated

Heat the butter in a heavy saucepan. Add the garlic and sauté until golden, then add the tomatoes, peppers, basil, salt, and pepper and simmer until the sauce thickens.

Cook the penne *al dente* (see page 26), then drain well. Toss with the cheeses and the sauce and serve.

Pasta con Piselli

This is a filling dish that makes a full meal with a plain green salad and garlic bread. The combination of salt pork and peas in this is very rich.

1 oz (30 g) salt pork, cubed
1 medium onion, finely chopped
2 cloves garlic, finely chopped
8 oz (250 g) fresh tomatoes, chopped
Salt and freshly ground black pepper to taste

1 teaspoon finely chopped fresh basil or ½ teaspoon dried
1 lb (500 g) fresh peas, shelled (or use 6 oz (180 g) frozen)
8 oz (250 g) spaghettini or ordinary spaghetti

Cook the pork in a heavy casserole until browned. Remove the browned bits with a slotted spoon and reserve; leave the fat in the casserole. Add the onion and garlic to the casserole and cook until wilted, then add the tomatoes, salt, pepper, and basil and simmer for 10 minutes.

Meanwhile, boil the peas in salted water for 5 to 8 minutes, or until just tender. Drain and add to the sauce.

Boil the pasta *al dente* (see page 26). Drain well, then toss with the sauce and salt pork bits and serve, offering freshly grated Parmesan cheese separately.

Rigatoni with Courgettes

Courgettes, properly cooked, which is *under*cooked, are delicious tossed with noodles. Use lots of freshly ground black pepper.

2 lb (1 kg) small courgettes	2 cloves garlic, very finely chopped
1 teaspoon salt	
1 lb (500 g) rigatoni	2 teaspoons finely chopped fresh thyme or 1 teaspoon dried
1 oz (30 g) butter	
2 tablespoons olive oil	Freshly ground black pepper to taste

Scrub the courgettes well and cut into thin strips the size of matchsticks. Salt and set aside for 1 hour, then drain and dry on paper towels.

Cook the rigatoni *al dente* (see page 26), then drain well.

Heat the butter and oil in a large frying pan until bubbling. Add the courgettes and sauté, stirring, for 2 minutes. Add the garlic and thyme and sauté for 1 minute longer.

Add pepper to the sauce, then toss with rigatoni and serve immediately with freshly grated Parmesan cheese.

Tagliatelle with Peas and Mushrooms

Tagliatelle with peas, cream and ham is a wonderful if common dish; but with peas and the pungent dried mushrooms and nutty fresh ones, a classic dish receives a pleasant twist.

2 tablespoons olive oil
1½ oz (45 g) butter
1 lb (500 g) fresh mushrooms, sliced
1 oz (30 g) dried Italian mushrooms,* soaked in warm water for 20 minutes, soaking water reserved (see note below)
2 cloves garlic, very finely chopped
2 lb (1 kg) fresh tagliatelle, home-made (see pages 22–3) or shop-bought*

2 egg yolks
½ pint (250 ml) double cream
1 lb (500 g) fresh peas, shelled and parboiled (or use 6 oz (180 g) frozen)
Salt and freshly ground black pepper
2 oz (60 g) Parmesan cheese, freshly grated
2 tablespoons chopped fresh parsley

Heat the oil and 1 oz (30 g) of the butter in a large frying pan. Add the fresh mushrooms and stir over a medium heat until the mushrooms start to exude their juices. Lower the heat, add the garlic, and simmer for 5 minutes.

Squeeze the soaked mushrooms dry, then slice and add to the frying pan. Stir for 2 minutes, then set aside.

Boil the tagliatelle *al dente* (see page 26), then drain. Place in a warm serving dish and toss with the remaining butter.

Add the egg yolks and cream to the mushrooms, stirring, then add the peas and stir over a *very* low heat until the mixture begins to thicken. Season with salt and pepper.

Toss the noodles and mushroom mixture lightly, together with the Parmesan cheese. Garnish with the parsley and serve at once.

Note: You can freeze the mushroom soaking liquid in a small plastic jar and use it for other sauces.

Spaghetti Ticino

Noodles tossed in cream, with various bits of bright vegetables and ham, are very attractive and easy to prepare. If you can use freshly made pasta, it is much better; the dried pasta seems better with heavier sauces.

2½ oz (75 g) butter

2 tablespoons olive oil

8 oz (250 g) fresh mushrooms, sliced

3 spring onions, very finely chopped

2 cloves garlic, very finely chopped

Salt and freshly ground pepper to taste

6 oz (190 g) ham, diced

½ pint (250 ml) single cream

1 lb (500 g) fresh tagliatelle, home-made (see pages 22–3) or shop-bought,* or spaghetti

½ medium bunch watercress, roughly chopped (about 8 tablespoons)

2 oz (60 g) Parmesan cheese, freshly grated

Heat 2 oz (60 g) of the butter and 1 tablespoon of the oil in a heavy frying pan, and sauté the mushrooms, stirring, over a medium high heat for 3 minutes.

Add the spring onions and garlic and stir-fry for 2 or 3 minutes more, then remove from the heat.

Heat the remaining butter and oil in a small frying pan. Add the ham and cook over a low heat. Add salt and pepper.

Add the cream to the mushroom mixture and return to the heat. Cook rapidly, to reduce the liquid, for 5 minutes.

Meanwhile, boil the pasta *al dente* (see page 26), then drain. Add to the mushroom mixture, along with the watercress, then turn off the heat and toss with the ham. Sprinkle with the cheese and serve immediately.

Pasta with Vegetables

Baked pasta dishes (*in forno*) are the only ones Italians consider main dishes. This is a baked version of *ratatouille* with pasta, and it can be frozen or refrigerated before baking.

2 oz (60 g) butter

2 tablespoons olive oil

2 medium onions, chopped

2 cloves garlic, finely chopped

1 tablespoon chopped fresh oregano or 1 teaspoon dried

1 tablespoon chopped fresh basil or 1 teaspoon dried

Salt and freshly ground black pepper to taste

4 tomatoes, peeled, seeded, and roughly chopped (see note on page 49)

4 small courgettes, scrubbed and sliced

¼ pint (125 ml) chicken stock, or more as needed

1 lb (500 g) small shells or elbow macaroni

2 oz (60 g) Parmesan cheese, freshly grated

Preheat the oven to 350°F (175°C), mark 4.

Heat 1 oz (30 g) of the butter and the oil in a heavy saucepan. Add the onion and garlic and sauté until golden, then add the oregano, basil, salt and pepper, tomatoes, courgettes, and chicken stock and simmer for 5 minutes, or until the courgettes are *just* tender.

Boil the pasta *al dente* (see page 26) and drain well. Toss with the vegetable mixture and place in a large, buttered casserole. Sprinkle the Parmesan over all, dot with the remaining butter and bake for 30 minutes, or until golden.

Spaghetti with Uncooked Basil and Tomato Sauce

One of my happiest noodle experiences was the discovery of the mixture of freshly cooked hot pasta with an uncooked vegetable sauce. Very summery and refreshing.

4 medium tomatoes, peeled, seeded and chopped (see note on page 49)

1 lb (500 g) mozzarella,* diced

8 tablespoons chopped fresh basil

2 cloves garlic, very finely chopped

8 fl oz (200 ml) olive oil

Salt and freshly ground black pepper to taste

1 lb (500 g) spaghetti

Combine the tomatoes, mozzarella, basil, garlic, oil, salt, and pepper and set aside for 1 hour.

Boil the spaghetti *al dente* (see page 26), then drain and toss with the tomato mixture. Serve immediately, offering freshly grated Parmesan cheese separately.

Pasta with Peppers

Garlicky peppers and tomatoes tossed with hot pasta and served with lemon – another example of an uncooked sauce for hot noodles. In this, as in other simple 'raw' sauces, the quality of the ingredients is an important factor. Ripe but not mushy tomatoes, *fresh* basil, and freshly grated cheese are essential.

6 medium tomatoes, sliced very thin

2 sweet red or yellow peppers, seeded and sliced into thin strips

8 tablespoons roughly chopped fresh basil

3 cloves garlic, finely chopped

Olive oil as needed – at least 4 tablespoons

Salt and freshly ground black pepper to taste

Freshly grated Parmesan or Romano pecorino cheese* to taste

1 lb (500 g) rigatoni or similar pasta

Lemon wedges for garnish

Combine the tomatoes, peppers, basil, garlic, oil, salt, and pepper and set aside.

Boil the pasta *al dente* (see page 26), then drain well, shaking. Toss with cheese to taste, more salt and pepper as needed, and the tomato mixture and serve with lemon wedges and more cheese.

Pasta with Dried and Fresh Mushrooms

These dried mushrooms are terribly expensive, but luckily an ounce or two goes a long way. In this recipe you soak the mushrooms in warm water. When you drain them for use in the recipe, be sure to save the liquid (I put it in small plastic jars and freeze it, and use it in other sauces).

2 oz (60 g) dried Italian mushrooms,* soaked in warm water
for 20 minutes, soaking liquid
reserved

1 lb (500 g) fresh mushrooms,
sliced

5 spring onions, chopped

8 tablespoons olive oil

2 sweet red or green peppers, cut
into thin shreds

2 cloves garlic, very finely
chopped

Salt and freshly ground black
pepper to taste

1 lb (500 g) ziti or rigatoni

Squeeze the soaked mushrooms dry, then slice and combine with all the other ingredients except the pasta. Set aside for 30 minutes to marinate.

Boil the pasta *al dente* (see page 26), then drain well and toss with the mushroom mixture. Serve immediately.

Shells with White Kidney Beans and Chick-peas

A nice white and red combination, this is similar to *pasta e fagioli* in nutritional value. Although, for simplicity's sake, I here give instructions for tinned chick-peas and kidney beans, I prefer dried (soaked overnight and boiled just until tender) because the tinned variety tend to be too mushy.

1 lb (500 g) small shells

2 tablespoons olive oil

1 large onion, chopped

2 cloves garlic, finely chopped

1 tablespoon chopped fresh basil
or 1 teaspoon dried

1 teaspoon dried oregano

½ teaspoon dried thyme

1 bay leaf

Salt and freshly ground black
pepper to taste

1 14 oz (440 g) tin Italian plum
tomatoes, blended until
smooth, mixed with 1 5 oz
(160 g) tin tomato paste

1½ tins (14 oz (440 g) size) chick-
peas

1½ tins (14 oz (440 g) size) cannellini (white kidney beans)

Boil the shells *al dente* (see page 26), then drain well.

Heat the oil in a saucepan. Sauté the onion and garlic in the oil until golden, then add the herbs, salt, pepper and tomato purée and simmer for 15 minutes. Add the chick-peas and cannellini and simmer for 15 minutes more.

Toss the sauce with the drained shells and serve immediately. Serve freshly grated Parmesan cheese separately.

Vermicelli with Mushroom Sauce

A very quick sauce in which mushrooms, anchovies, and, surprisingly, mint combine deliciously. (Mint is, after all, a cousin to basil.)

2 tablespoons olive oil	small tin (8 oz (250 g) size),
3 cloves garlic, finely chopped	drained and chopped
1 tin (2 oz (60 g)) anchovies,	½ teaspoon chopped fresh mint or
drained and chopped	¼ teaspoon dried
8 oz (250 g) fresh mushrooms,	1 teaspoon salt
sliced	½ teaspoon freshly ground black
1 large tin (28 oz (875 g) size)	pepper
Italian plum tomatoes, plus 1	1 lb (500 g) vermicelli

Heat the oil in a frying pan, then add the garlic, anchovies, mushrooms, tomatoes, mint, salt, and pepper. Cook for 10 minutes over a medium high flame, stirring frequently.

Meanwhile, boil the vermicelli *al dente* (see page 26). Drain, put into a serving dish, and pour the sauce over. Serve immediately.

Spinach and Tagliatelle in Cream

In my opinion, spinach is best after it has absorbed three times its weight in butter – a rather extravagant French method of dealing with it – or cooked very quickly in olive oil and garlic, a basic Sicilian practice. It also has a natural affinity for cream, and tossed with tagliatelle is quite delicious.

1 lb (500 g) fresh spinach, cleaned (with tough stems removed) and chopped
2 cloves garlic, very finely chopped
1 small onion, very finely chopped
3 tablespoons olive oil
1 oz (30 g) butter
1 lb (500 g) spinach tagliatelle
½ pint (250 ml) double cream
Salt and freshly ground black pepper to taste

In a large, heavy saucepan, sauté the garlic and onion in the oil and half the butter until golden. Put in the spinach, cover tightly, and let cook over a low heat until just wilted.

Meanwhile, boil the tagliatelle *al dente* (see page 26). Drain and toss with the remaining butter, then toss with the spinach and the cream in the saucepan. Heat the pasta through, then season with salt and pepper and serve, offering freshly grated Parmesan cheese separately.

Pasta alla Caponata

Caponata, which this recipe resembles, is a cold aubergine mixture often served in antipasto courses. It is best made ahead, as is this delicious pasta sauce.

2 cloves garlic, very finely chopped
4 tablespoons olive oil
1 sweet red pepper, diced
1 sweet green pepper, diced
1½ lb (750 g) aubergine, peeled and cubed
15 black olives, chopped
8 tomatoes, peeled, seeded, and chopped (see note on page 49)
½ tin (2 oz (60 g) size) anchovies, chopped
1 tablespoon chopped fresh basil or 1 teaspoon dried
1 teaspoon capers
Salt and freshly ground black pepper to taste
1 lb (500 g) spaghetti or other pasta

Sauté the garlic in the olive oil for 3 minutes, then add the peppers, aubergine, and olives and simmer for 15 minutes. Add the tomatoes, anchovies, basil, and capers and simmer for 15 minutes longer, then add salt and pepper to taste.

Cook the pasta *al dente* (see page 26). Drain, put into a serving dish, and pour the sauce over. Serve immediately, offering freshly grated Parmesan cheese separately.

Baked Aubergine with Pasta

A layered pasta version of aubergine *parmigiana*. Before baking, this dish can be covered with foil and frozen. It is excellent for large crowds.

2 medium aubergines, peeled and sliced

2 tablespoons salt

8 tablespoons or more olive oil or olive and corn oils, mixed

2 cloves garlic, finely chopped

1½ lb (750 g) tomatoes, peeled, seeded, and chopped (see note on page 49)

2 teaspoons chopped fresh basil or 1 teaspoon dried

Freshly ground pepper to taste

1 lb (500 g) medium macaroni, boiled *al dente* (see page 26) and drained

8 oz (250 g) mozzarella,* sliced thin

2 oz (60 g) Parmesan cheese, freshly grated

Preheat the oven to 325°F (160°C), mark 3.

Toss the aubergine slices in the salt and put in a colander to drain for 30 minutes.

Heat the oil in a large frying pan and brown the aubergine slices, a few at a time, adding more oil as needed and removing the aubergine to a plate as done.

Add 2 tablespoons of oil to the frying pan and sauté the garlic until golden. Add the tomatoes and basil and simmer for 15 minutes, adding water if necessary to make a medium thick sauce.

In a buttered casserole, layer the macaroni, aubergine, and tomatoes and top with the cheeses. Bake for 30 minutes, or until the cheeses brown.

Pasta Marinara

Marinara sauce is really a basic tomato sauce with (preferably) fresh herbs. Traditionally it is said to be the simple tomato sauce in which fishermen (hence 'marinara') would cook seafood on board their boats. It is best made just before using.

1 large (28 oz (875 g) size) tin Italian plum tomatoes, drained and roughly chopped, or 2 lb (1 kg) fresh tomatoes, peeled, seeded, and chopped (see note on page 49)
3 tablespoons olive oil
4 medium onions, finely chopped
2 cloves garlic, very finely chopped

Salt and freshly ground black pepper to taste
1 tablespoon chopped fresh oregano or 1 teaspoon dried
1 tablespoon chopped fresh basil or 1 teaspoon dried
1 bay leaf
1 lb (500 g) spaghetti or any medium-sized pasta

Put the tomatoes, tinned or fresh, through a food mill and set aside.

Heat the oil in a heavy saucepan and sauté the onion until golden, stirring occasionally. Add the garlic and sauté for 2 minutes more, then add the tomatoes, salt, pepper, and herbs and simmer for 30 minutes, partially covered.

Boil the pasta *al dente* (see page 26). Drain well, put into a serving bowl, and serve with the sauce. Serve freshly grated Parmesan cheese separately.

Spinach Sformato with Pasta

A sformato is a baked egg dish, usually with vegetables. This one uses the combination of bacon and spinach.

2 oz (60 g) butter
1 medium onion, finely chopped

3 lb (1½ kg) spinach, washed and cooked rapidly in the water clinging to the leaves

Salt and freshly ground pepper to taste

4 rashers bacon, fried and crumbled

3 tablespoons freshly grated Parmesan cheese

1 tablespoon plain flour

8 fl oz (200 ml) milk, heated

3 eggs

2 oz (60 g) macaroni, cooked and drained

Preheat the oven to 350°F (175°C), mark 4.

Heat 1 oz (30 g) of the butter in a heavy frying pan and sauté the onion until golden. Add the spinach, finely chopped, then season with salt and pepper and add the bacon and Parmesan.

In a separate pan, heat the remaining 1 oz (30 g) butter and add the flour, stirring well. Add the milk very slowly, whisking to keep the sauce smooth as it thickens. Let cool a little, then add the egg yolks, one at a time, and salt and pepper to taste. Add this bechamel sauce and the cooked macaroni to the vegetable mixture.

Beat the egg whites until stiff and fold gently into the vegetables. Place in a buttered soufflé dish or casserole and bake until bubbly and brown, about 1 hour. Serve with grilled foods, or on its own with a mushroom sauce.

Tortellini with Spinach and Ricotta Filling

Tortellini are to some the height of *pasta ripieni*, or stuffed pasta. The Bolognese call them 'navels of Venus', and there are many

stories concerning their origin. One has an enamoured cook moulding the pasta to fit his lover's navel, in another the inventor has a vision of Venus, and copies her navel . . . No matter whose navel inspired them, they are delicious – best, I think, tossed in heated double cream and Parmesan.

8 oz (250 g) fresh spinach, washed and picked over

2 oz (60 g) butter or margarine

3 medium onions, finely chopped

6 slices ham, finely chopped

8 oz (250 g) ricotta cheese*

2 oz (60 g) Romano* or Parmesan cheese, freshly grated

Freshly grated nutmeg, salt, and

freshly ground black pepper to taste

Fresh Egg Pasta (pages 21–3), made and set aside under a cloth while preparing the filling

½ pint (250 ml) double cream

Freshly grated Parmesan cheese to taste

Place the spinach in a saucepan with water still clinging to the leaves, and cover tightly. Cook over a medium heat just until wilted, then drain in a colander, pressing to remove all the water. Chop finely and set aside.

Heat the butter or margarine in a heavy frying pan. Add the onion and cook, stirring occasionally, until golden. Add the ham and spinach and cook, stirring, for a few minutes. Add the ricotta, Romano or Parmesan, nutmeg, salt, and pepper.

Cut the dough into four portions. Using one at a time (cover the others), roll out to a thickness of about ⅛ inch (3 mm). (If the dough is too springy, let it rest longer.) Cut out circles about 2 inches (5 cm) in diameter with a glass or a round cutter.

Place a small amount of filling in the centre of each circle, then fold over in a half-moon shape and pinch the edges tightly together. Draw the ends across the centre and pinch together in a ring.

As you make them, place them, not touching, on a clean cloth and cover. Let them dry out a little for an hour or so. (The dough must be worked before it dries out, however, so work quickly.) Repeat with the other three portions of dough.

At serving time, bring a large saucepan of water to the boil and boil the tortellini for about 5 minutes, or until done (try one). Drain and keep warm in a serving dish.

Meanwhile, heat the cream carefully with Parmesan to taste and a little salt and pepper. Pour over the tortellini, toss, and serve at once.

Pasta e Fagioli I

Pasta e fagioli, like some other grain and vegetable combinations (the Nepali rice and lentil curry, for instance) provides a good protein-rich meal, for the protein of the beans is augmented by the catalytic action of the pasta. Anyway, the dish is delicious.

1 shin of beef (about 2 lb (1 kg))
1 lb (500 g) small white beans, soaked overnight and drained
2 tablespoons olive oil
3 cloves garlic, very finely chopped
1 tablespoon chopped fresh basil or 1 teaspoon dried
Salt and freshly ground black pepper to taste

5 medium tomatoes, peeled, seeded, and chopped (see note on page 49)
1 tablespoon tomato paste
1 lb (500 g) small macaroni
2 tablespoons chopped fresh parsley
Freshly grated Parmesan cheese

Place the beef in a large saucepan and add the drained beans. Cover with cold water and simmer, skimming off the scum, until the beans are tender. Remove from the heat.

Heat the oil in a frying pan and sauté the garlic until brown. Add the basil, salt, pepper, tomatoes, and tomato paste and cook gently for 5 minutes. Add to the beans.

Cook the macaroni *al dente* (see page 26); drain and add to the beans. Pour out any extra liquid and save the beef for another dish. Simmer for 5 minutes to heat through, then serve, topped with the parsley and Parmesan.

Pasta e Fagioli II

Of course, the variations on this classic dish are endless. This one is made with dry lentils, so it requires more cooking time, since they aren't presoaked, but long simmering makes them absorb flavours well.

4 rashers bacon	1½ pints (750 ml) water, more if necessary
2 onions, roughly chopped	
2 cloves garlic, very finely chopped	12 oz (375 g) dried red or brown lentils
1 carrot, scraped and chopped	2 bay leaves
1 sweet green pepper, seeded and chopped	2 teaspoons dried thyme
	1 tablespoon dried oregano
1 tin (14 oz (440 g)) Italian plum tomatoes, drained and roughly chopped	1 tablespoon dried basil
	1 lb (500 g) spaghettini or ordinary spaghetti

Sauté the bacon in a large, heavy saucepan. When crisp, add the onions, garlic, carrots, and green pepper. When the onions are golden, add the tomatoes and water and bring to the boil. Reduce to a simmer, then add the lentils gradually, stirring constantly. Add the herbs and simmer for ½ hour or more, until the lentils are tender.

Add the pasta and more water, if necessary. Cook for 8 minutes more, or until the pasta is cooked *al dente*. Serve in bowls, offering freshly grated Parmesan cheese separately.

Pasta with Peperonata

Sweet peppers add colour and texture, as well as flavour, to a tomato sauce. Take special care not to overcook them and lose their texture and fresh taste in the process.

1 tablespoon olive oil	2 cloves garlic, finely chopped
1 oz (30 g) butter	6 large ripe tomatoes, peeled, seeded, and roughly chopped (see note on page 49)
1 medium onion, roughly chopped	
4 sweet red peppers, seeded and cut in thin strips	
1 sweet green pepper, seeded and cut in strips	12 oz (375 g) ziti or rigatoni

Heat the oil and butter in a saucepan and sauté the onion until lightly browned. Add the peppers, cover the pan, and simmer for 10 minutes over a low heat, then add the garlic and tomatoes and simmer, covered, for another 30 minutes. (If the mixture is too liquid, simmer with the cover off.)

Boil the pasta *al dente* (see page 26), then drain well. Toss with the *peperonata* and serve. Serve freshly grated Parmesan cheese separately.

Tagliatelle con Aspergi

Freshly cooked asparagus, tossed in cream and lightly seasoned, is a delicious accompaniment to fresh pasta.

2 oz (60 g) butter
2 cloves garlic, mashed
1 lb (500 g) asparagus, stems peeled, cut in 1-inch (2- or 3-cm) pieces
½ pint (250 ml) double cream
1 lb (500 g) tagliatelle, preferably fresh, either homemade (see pages 22–3) or shop-bought
Salt and freshly ground black pepper to taste
2 oz (60 g) Parmesan cheese, freshly grated

Heat the butter in a heavy frying pan. Stir-fry the garlic in the butter until golden, then add the asparagus and cream and simmer gently, just until the asparagus is tender.

Boil the tagliatelle *al dente* (see page 26) and drain well. Season the asparagus with salt and pepper and toss with the tagliatelle, then serve sprinkled with the Parmesan.

Spaghetti Zaccharia

This is named after the best six-year-old spaghetti eater I know, Zachary Bell. His favourite is *pesto*, but this was already taken. The sauce is also called 'tomato *piccante*'.

2 tablespoons olive oil
3 large sweet red peppers, seeded and chopped
3 medium tomatoes, peeled, seeded and chopped (see note on page 49)
3 cloves garlic, very finely chopped

1 tin (2 oz (60 g)) anchovies, chopped
1 tablespoon capers
Salt and freshly ground black pepper to taste
Lemon juice to taste
1 lb (500 g) spaghetti

Heat the olive oil in a frying pan. Sauté the peppers briefly, then add the tomatoes, garlic, anchovies, capers, and salt and pepper. Simmer for 5 minutes.

Boil the spaghetti *al dente* (see page 26) and drain well. Add the lemon juice to the sauce, toss with the spaghetti and serve immediately. Serve freshly grated Romano cheese* separately.

Gemelli Milanese

I'm very fond of these gemelli ('twins'), for they hold on to the sauce well. It is interesting to see that these and other more recondite macaroni forms like fusilli are becoming more common.

4 rashers bacon
1 small onion, finely chopped
8 oz (250 g) fresh mushrooms, sliced
1 14 oz (440 g) tin Italian plum tomatoes, roughly chopped

4 sweet green peppers, seeded and chopped
Salt and freshly ground black pepper to taste
1 teaspoon dry mustard
1 lb (500 g) gemelli

Sauté the bacon in a heavy frying pan. Drain off the extra fat, leaving 2 tablespoons. Add the onion and sauté until golden, then add the mushrooms and sauté until wilted. Add the tomatoes, peppers, salt, pepper, and mustard and cook for 15 minutes.

Boil the gemelli *al dente* (see page 26), then drain and toss with the vegetable mixture. Serve at once, offering freshly grated Romano cheese* separately.

Noodles with Sauerkraut

This Belgian dish is quite robust and has a wonderful aroma. It is also attractive: a moulded ham-noodle dish surrounded by seasoned sauerkraut simmered in Moselle.

1 lb (500 g) fresh sauerkraut (rinsed and drained in a colander)
¼ pint (125 ml) Moselle or other dry white wine
4 juniper berries
1 bay leaf
1 teaspoon caraway seeds
2 dried red chillies,* chopped
Salt and freshly ground black pepper to taste

1 lb (500 g) wide egg noodles
½ oz (15 g) butter
3 tablespoons breadcrumbs
12 oz (375 g) ordinary ham, smoked ham or Polish sausage, chopped
3 eggs
½ pint (250 ml) milk

Preheat oven to 300°F (150°C), mark 2.

In a saucepan, simmer sauerkraut with wine, juniper berries, bay leaf, chillies and salt and pepper for about 20 minutes.

Boil noodles for 7 minutes or *al dente*. Drain noodles in a colander and run water through them. Use the butter to butter a 2-pint (1-litre) mould and shake breadcrumbs to coat the inside. Alternate noodles and ham until almost full. Pour milk and eggs, beaten together, over noodles. Cover mould and bake for 1 hour. Turn the mould out on to a serving dish. Surround with well-drained sauerkraut and serve.

Curried Cauliflower with Raisins and Vermicelli

An unusual combination, but surprisingly delicious. I think of it as a barebones curry without the heat, but with the interesting counterpoints of sweet (raisins) and sour (lime juice), crunchiness (sesame seeds) and smoothness (cauliflower).

2 medium onions, sliced	1–2 oz (30–60 g) raisins
3 tablespoons mustard oil* or groundnut oil	Generous ½ pint (250 ml) chicken stock
1 teaspoon sesame seeds	1 tablespoon lime juice
2 teaspoons cumin	1 teaspoon granulated sugar
2 teaspoons finely chopped fresh ginger*	Salt to taste
1 cauliflower, cut into florets	1 lb (500 g) vermicelli

Sauté the sliced onions in 2 tablespoons of the oil until soft. Add the sesame seeds, cumin, and ginger and sauté for a few more minutes. Add the cauliflower and rasins, then pour in the chicken stock, cover, and simmer for about 10 minutes, until the cauliflower is just tender. Add the lime juice, sugar, and salt to taste.

Meanwhile, boil the vermicelli *al dente* (see page 26) and drain. Heat the remaining tablespoon of oil in a wok, add the vermicelli, and stir-fry over a high heat for 5 minutes. Top the pasta with the cauliflower mixture and serve.

Mee Rebus

Bean sprouts and hot 'curry' ingredients make this Malaysian noodle dish a meeting place of the Chinese and Indian noodle traditions.

8 dried red chillies*	1 tablespoon ground coriander
5 spring onions, finely chopped	1 teaspoon ground anise
2 tablespoons finely chopped fresh ginger*	1 teaspoon ground cumin
	½ teaspoon ground turmeric

3 tablespoons mustard oil* or
  groundnut oil
1 beef or chicken bouillon cube
¾ pint (375 ml) water
2 medium potatoes, boiled,
  peeled, and mashed

1 lb (500 g) thin egg noodles
12 oz (375 g) bean sprouts
2–3 oz (60–90 g) dry-roasted peanuts (roasted without oil – use
  ordinary roasted nuts if you
  can't find them)

Grind or pound the chillies, spring onions, and ginger together. Combine with the coriander, aniseed, cumin, and turmeric and set aside.

Heat the oil in a heavy frying pan until it smokes. Add the bouillon cube and water and simmer for 2 minutes. Stir in the mashed potatoes.

Boil the noodles *al dente* (see page 26), then drain and place in a serving dish. Add the bean sprouts, sauce, and peanuts, and toss well before serving.

Szechuan Noodles
(Vegetable Version)

This version of Szechuan noodles combines bean sprouts, spinach, and noodles in a typically spicy cold sauce that includes sesame paste or peanut butter. A similar Szechuan dish with chicken is also included (see page 183).

1 lb (500 g) fresh Chinese egg
  noodles* or fresh Soya Bean
  Noodles (see page 24)
2 tablespoons groundnut oil
3 tablespoons soy sauce*
1 tablespoon vinegar
2 teaspoons chilli paste with
  garlic* or Tabasco to taste
  mixed with 2 cloves garlic, very
  finely chopped

2 tablespoons sesame paste* or
  peanut butter
1 tablespoon sesame oil*
¼ pint (125 ml) chicken stock
8 oz (250 g) fresh bean sprouts,
  washed and picked over
6 oz (190 g) fresh spinach,
  roughly chopped

Boil the noodles *al dente* – about 5 minutes, less for the soya bean noodles. Drain well.

Heat the groundnut oil in a large wok. Toss the noodles in the oil until they are heated through and beginning to brown.

Combine the soy sauce, vinegar, chilli paste, sesame paste, sesame oil, and stock in a serving bowl and mix well. Add the noodles, bean sprouts, and spinach and toss well. Serve immediately.

Curried Vegetables
with Egg Vermicelli

Many Indian dishes, though not originally served with noodles, go very well with them. This is a colourful vegetable curry.

2 medium onions, finely chopped
2 tablespoons mustard oil* or groundnut oil
1 tablespoon very finely chopped fresh ginger*
1 tablespoon very finely chopped garlic
1 teaspoon whole fenugreek seed*
2 teaspoons ground turmeric
1 teaspoon ground coriander
1 teaspoon ground cumin
1 teaspoon hot paprika or kashmiri mirsch*
1 teaspoon salt
½ teaspoon pounded dried red chillies*

¼ teaspoon ground cinnamon
5 courgettes, scrubbed and sliced
1 small aubergine, peeled and cubed
1 sweet green pepper, seeded and sliced
3 medium tomatoes, peeled, seeded, and chopped (see note on page 49)
1 carrot, scraped and sliced
1 tablespoon groundnut oil
1 lb (500 g) egg vermicelli, fresh Chinese* or dried

Sauté the onion in the 2 tablespoons oil in a large frying pan. Add the ginger, the garlic, all the spices, and the salt and sauté until the garlic is soft, about 5 minutes. Add all the vegetables and cook, covered, until soft, about 30 minutes.

Boil fresh noodles for about 5 minutes or cook dried ones *al dente* (see page 26), then drain. Heat the groundnut oil in a wok or frying pan and toss the cooked noodles in it until they begin to brown. Serve the vegetables on a nest of noodles.

Noodles with Mangetouts
and Baby Corn

Peas and corn, both ordinary vegetables in our cooking, appear together in this dish in unusual forms. Have all the ingredients measured and ready so that the dish may be assembled very quickly and the vegetables retain their crispness.

½ lb (250 g) mangetouts, trimmed and washed
1 tin (15 oz (470 g)) baby corn*
1 lb (500 g) spaghetti or fresh Chinese flat noodles*
2 tablespoons groundnut oil
3 spring onions, chopped

2 tablespoons soy sauce*
½ teaspoon granulated sugar
1 teaspoon sesame oil*
½ teaspoon red wine vinegar
3 tablespoons oyster sauce*
1 tablespoon cornflour dissolved in 4 tablespoons water

Blanch the mangetouts by pouring boiling water over them in a colander; follow with cold water and drain well. Drain the baby corn.

Cook the noodles *al dente* (see page 26) and drain. Heat the ground-nut oil in a wok, add the drained noodles, and stir-fry until some are browned. Add the spring onions, soy sauce, sugar, and sesame oil and continue stirring. Add the mangetouts and corn.

Combine the vinegar, the oyster sauce and the cornflour and water mixture, and add, stirring, to the noodles. Serve at once, with extra soy sauce if desired.

Cold Soba with Bean Curd

Soba, the light green buckwheat noodles, are commonly served cold in the summer. With cubes of bean curd, they are a favourite treat in Japan.

1 lb (500 g) soba noodles★	1 tablespoon rice wine vinegar★
2 squares bean curd,★ cut into ½-inch (1-cm) cubes	1 tablespoon soy sauce
3 spring onions, chopped	½ teaspoon granulated sugar
2 tablespoons sesame seeds, toasted carefully in a frying pan	½ teaspoon salt
1 teaspoon sesame oil★	½ teaspoon aonoriko (dried, pulverized seaweed)★ (optional)

Cook the noodles *al dente* (see page 26), then drain in a colander and cool by running cold water through them. Place in a bowl of cold water in the refrigerator until almost ready to serve.

Place the cold noodles, drained, in a serving bowl and top with the bean curd cubes, spring onions, and toasted sesame seeds.

Combine the remaining ingredients. Just before serving, pour the sauce over the noodles and toss very lightly.

Note: This is a dish meant to be 'slurped' up: the noise of eating noodles in Japan is perfectly good manners!

Japanese Summer Somen

The *soba-ya* (noodle restaurants) of Japan serve some wonderful steamy noodles in the winter, but in the summer they produce lovely cooling noodle dishes. These, with a vegetable garnish, are served with ice cubes.

1 lb (500 g) somen (wheat
   noodles)*

Sauce

6 tablespoons light soy sauce*
2 teaspoons rice wine vinegar*
2 tablespoons granulated sugar

1 teaspoon sesame oil*
½ pint (250 ml) defatted chicken
   stock

Garnishes (to taste)

Sansho pepper* or togarashi (hot
   red pepper)*
Chopped fresh coriander
Chopped spring onion

Cucumber shreds
Spicy Japanese pickled vege-
   tables*
Shredded fresh ginger*

Boil the noodles *al dente* (see page 26), then drain in a colander and cool by running cold water through them. Set aside in a bowl of cold water in the refrigerator until almost ready to serve.

Heat the sauce ingredients just enough to dissolve the sugar, then chill.

Just before serving, drain the noodles and divide between 6 bowls. Arrange your choice of garnishes over the noodles and pour the sauce over each. Serve with an ice cube in each bowl.

Tibetan Tomato Sauce with Noodles

Khancha, the Tibetan cook of a friend in Nepal, would serve us delicious *momos*, meat-filled dumplings, with this sauce. She also said it was good with thin egg noodles, a staple Tibetan food, and it is.

2 tablespoons mustard oil* or
   groundnut oil
1 small onion, finely chopped

1 teaspoon fenugreek seed*
4 tomatoes, peeled, seeded, and
   chopped (see note on page 49)

Cayenne pepper to taste

3 tablespoons chopped fresh coriander or 1 teaspoon ground coriander

Salt to taste

1 lb (500 g) fine egg noodles, fresh Chinese* or dried

Heat the oil in a saucepan and sauté the onion until golden. Add the fenugreek seed and sauté, stirring, for 3 minutes longer. Add the chopped tomatoes, coriander, cayenne, and salt, and simmer, partially covered, for 30 minutes. (If the sauce dries out, add a little water.) Serve over the noodles, boiled *al dente* (see page 26).

Fried Indian Noodles
with Vegetable Garnishes

A halfway recipe that shows the crossed noodle paths of India and China. The vegetables are to be crisp like Chinese vegetables, yet the combination, with garnishes, is quite Indian. Still, it seems more appropriate to eat it with chopsticks!

1 lb (500 g) egg noodles, fresh Chinese* or dried

1 tablespoon mustard oil* or vegetable oil

5 tablespoons groundnut oil

8 oz (250 g) green beans, ends removed and sliced into 1-inch (2- or 3-cm) pieces

3 oz (90 g) shelled peas

8 oz (250 g) cabbage, finely shredded

2 tablespoons shredded fresh ginger*

3 fresh green chillies, shredded

4 spring onions, chopped

Salt and freshly ground pepper to taste

¾ pint (375 ml) corn oil for deep frying

3 tablespoons chopped fresh coriander or 1 teaspoon ground coriander

3 tablespoons sliced, roasted almonds

3 oz (90 g) raisins, sautéed briefly in 1 oz (30 g) butter

Boil the egg noodles *al dente* (see page 26), then toss with the mustard or vegetable oil and let cool.

Heat the groundnut oil in a frying pan. Add the beans, peas, cabbage, ginger, and chillies, in turn, frying over high heat for 2 or

3 minutes, and stirring well each time a vegetable is added. Add the spring onions, toss, and remove from the heat. Add salt and pepper to taste.

In a large frying pan or wok, heat the corn oil to 350°F (175°C) on a deep-frying thermometer and fry the noodles in handfuls, removing the paper towels when crisp and golden. Place the noodles on a serving dish and top with the mixed vegetables. Garnish with the coriander, almonds, and raisins and serve.

Note: If you do not have a thermometer test the oil with a noodle or a small cube of bread. If it browns in 60 seconds it is hot enough. If the oil smokes it is too hot and the noodles will burn.

Korean Noodles with Pine Nuts

Korean noodle dishes have a subtle sweetness. This one is excellent served with grilled foods, like the famous *bul kogi* – grilled beef strips with sesame seeds and garlic.

8 oz (250 g) very thin vermicelli, broken into bits
2 tablespoons groundnut oil
2–3 oz (60–90 g) almond flakes
4 oz (125 g) pine nuts*
2 tablespoons honey
2 tablespoons soy sauce

Boil the vermicelli *al dente* (see page 26) and drain well.

Heat the oil in a heavy frying pan and brown the almonds and pine nuts in it, stirring. Add to the vermicelli along with the honey and soy sauce, tossing with forks. Serve immediately.

Baingan Tamatar (Aubergine and Tomato Curry with Noodles)

Although a 'curry', this dish has no 'curry' spices. It is a relatively light vegetable mixture with browned noodles. It should, however, be 'hot' with cayenne and chillies.

1 lb (500 g) very thin egg noodles
1 large aubergine (about 1 lb (500 g))
Salt
1 oz (30 g) butter or 2 tablespoons mustard oil*
2 medium onions, thinly sliced
1 sweet green pepper, seeded and diced
½ teaspoon freshly ground black pepper

½ teaspoon cayenne pepper
6 ripe tomatoes, peeled, seeded, and sliced (see note on page 49)
2 fresh green chillies, shredded (optional)
2 tablespoons vegetable oil
2 tablespoons chopped fresh coriander or parsley

Boil the noodles *al dente* (see page 26), then drain and let cool.

Peel the aubergine, then cut into small chunks. Sprinkle with 1 tablespoon salt and let stand in a colander, over a bowl or sink, for 30 minutes. Dry on paper towels.

Heat the butter or oil in a large frying pan and stir-fry the onion and green pepper until the onion is golden. Add the black pepper and cayenne and stir, then add the aubergine. Cover and cook over a slow heat until almost tender.

Add the tomatoes, chillies, and salt to taste, then cover and cook, stirring frequently, until the tomatoes and aubergine are done.

Heat the vegetable oil in a wok. Add the cooled noodles and fry, stirring, over a high heat until some are browned. Place the noodles in a serving bowl and toss with the aubergine mixture. Garnish with the fresh coriander or parsley and serve.

Burmese Tomato Curry
with Noodles

Burmese food is, unfortunately, little known in this country. It combines aspects of both Indian and Chinese cooking, but emphasizes special tastes, like deep-fried garlic and fish sauce, which distinguish it from these more familiar cuisines. The recipe below presents a delightful version of tomato sauce.

3 lb (1½ kg) tomatoes, peeled, seeded, and chopped (see note on page 49)

3 tablespoons groundnut or mustard oil★

4 medium onions, very thinly sliced

3 cloves garlic, very finely chopped

Salt to taste

1 teaspoon ground turmeric

1 teaspoon ground coriander

½ teaspoon crushed dried red chillies★

1 tablespoon fish sauce★

12 oz (375 g) thin egg noodles

Heat the oil in a heavy saucepan. Add the sliced onion and garlic and sauté until golden; then add the tomatoes, salt, turmeric, coriander, chillies and fish sauce and cook over a very low heat for 20 to 30 minutes.

Boil the noodles *al dente* (see page 26), then drain well, toss with the tomato mixture, and serve.

Fideos con Salsa de nuez

An Argentinian recipe which reminds me of a walnut pesto, but with refinements: the crème fraîche at the beginning, and the essential homemade egg noodles. Quite a filling dish.

2 lb (1 kg) noodles, made from Fresh Egg Pasta (see pages 22–4)

4 tablespoons each sour cream and double cream, mixed

Salt and freshly ground black pepper

1½ oz (45 g) butter

2 cloves garlic, very finely chopped

4 oz (125 g) walnuts, finely chopped

4 oz (125 g) Parmesan cheese, freshly grated

¼ pint (250 ml) chicken stock

Boil the noodles *al dente* (see page 26), then drain well and toss with the mixed creams (an approximation of crème fraîche, which you should use instead if you have it), salt and pepper to taste, and 1 oz (30 g) of the butter. Cover and keep warm.

Heat the remaining ½ oz (15 g) butter in a small saucepan. Sauté the garlic for 3 minutes; be careful not to let it brown. Remove from the heat, then stir in the walnuts, Parmesan, and chicken stock, and toss with the noodles. Serve immediately.

Mushroom Casserole with Pasta

Mushrooms, baked with pasta, are quite delicious. Like other casserole noodle dishes, this one can be assembled ahead of time and baked later. It can even be frozen before baking.

2 oz (60 g) butter
6 oz (190 g) fresh mushrooms, sliced
2 teaspoons lemon juice
1 clove garlic, very finely chopped
1 oz (30 g) Parmesan cheese, freshly grated
Salt and freshly ground pepper to taste

8 oz (250 g) rotini or other macaroni
2 eggs, lightly beaten
8 fl oz (200 ml) milk
½ oz (15 g) plain flour
½ oz (15 g) breadcrumbs

Preheat the oven to 375°F (190°C), mark 5.

Melt half the butter in a frying pan. Add the mushrooms and cook, stirring, for 5 minutes, then add the lemon juice, garlic, Parmesan, and salt and pepper to taste. Set aside.

Boil the pasta *al dente* (see page 26). Drain well.

In a bowl combine the eggs, milk, flour, and salt and pepper to taste. Beat well, then combine with the mushrooms and fold into the pasta. Pour into a buttered casserole. Sprinkle with the breadcrumbs and dot with the remaining butter. Bake in the preheated oven for 30 minutes, or until bubbly and browned.

Ratatouille with Noodles

Ratatouille is a wonderful summer staple. Good cold or hot, it is splendid on noodles and improves upon a day or two's rest in the refrigerator. With aubergine, courgettes, and tomatoes as a base, you can experiment by adding other vegetables in season. *Ratatouille* reminds me of a one-shot *Rumtopf*, that endless alcoholic pot to which one adds fruits as they ripen all summer to make a pungent compote by the autumn.

1 medium aubergine, peeled and cut into small cubes

3 medium courgettes, scrubbed and sliced

Salt

6 tablespoons olive oil

3 onions, coarsely chopped

2 green peppers, seeded and diced

3 cloves garlic, very finely chopped

1 bay leaf

2 lb (1 kg) ripe tomatoes, peeled, seeded, and chopped (see note on page 49)

1 bunch fresh parsley, chopped (about 8 tablespoons)

½ teaspoon dried thyme

1 tablespoon chopped fresh basil or 1 teaspoon dried

1 lb (500 g) egg noodles

Place the aubergine and courgettes in a large colander over the sink or a saucepan. Salt well and toss, then leave to drain for 1 hour.

Heat the oil in a large frying pan or saucepan. Sauté the onion and green pepper until the onion is golden, then add the garlic, bay leaf, and tomatoes and simmer for 10 minutes. Add the aubergine and courgettes, after rinsing with cold water and patting dry. Simmer for 10 minutes, then add the parsley, thyme, and basil and simmer for 20 minutes more.

Boil the noodles *al dente* (see page 26), then drain. Toss with the *ratatouille* mixture and serve.

Black Beans and Macaroni

This much garlic may seem like a lot, but in the cooking it loses its pungency and adds a very savoury nuttiness to the rich bean and macaroni combination. I'm not sure of this recipe's ethnic origins, but it is probably from the southern United States or from Central America.

12 oz (375 g) dried black beans, soaked overnight and drained

1 head garlic, separated into cloves, then peeled and very finely chopped

8 oz (250 g) salt pork, finely diced

1 lb (500 g) elbow macaroni or small shells

1 tablespoon ground cumin

1 tablespoon salt

Freshly ground pepper to taste

Cook the beans slowly, in water to cover, adding 2 cloves of the garlic, until tender. Drain, saving the liquid.

Preheat the oven to 325°F (160°C), mark 3.

Sauté the salt pork in a heavy frying pan until crisp and golden. Remove with a slotted spoon on to paper towels. Add the remaining garlic to the fat in the frying pan and sauté over a very low heat, until soft.

Boil the noodles *al dente* (see page 26), then drain and toss with the beans, together with the salt pork and garlic, cumin, salt, and pepper. Pour into a casserole, add a little of the liquid from the beans, then bake in the oven, covered, for about an hour.

Green Noodle Soufflé

If you can find green vermicelli, use it. Otherwise the green will come from the spinach, parsley, and spring onions in the recipe. This makes a substantial vegetable dish to plan a meal around.

8 oz (250 g) vermicelli

1¼ lb (625 g) frozen spinach, defrosted, drained, and finely chopped

1 bunch fresh parsley, chopped (about 8 tablespoons)

4 tablespoons spring onions, finely chopped

4 oz (125 g) Parmesan cheese, freshly grated

2 oz (60 g) butter, melted

Salt and freshly ground black pepper to taste

4 eggs, separated

Preheat the oven to 350°F (175°C), mark 4.

Break the vermicelli into small pieces and boil *al dente* (see page 26). Drain well.

Combine the spinach, parsley, spring onions, drained vermicelli, Parmesan, butter, salt, pepper and egg yolks.

Beat the egg whites until stiff, then, very gently, fold them into the spinach mixture. Pour into a greased casserole and bake for 40 minutes, or until set and browned.

Vegetable Spaghetti

This dish is an improvisation of two graduate students who found that their budget called for many meatless meals. I used ordinary spaghetti when I made it, but I'm sure it would also be delicious with a short broad noodle, or with shells.

1 lb (500 g) spaghetti	1 oz (30 g) butter
1 lb (500 g) broccoli, washed and separated into small florets	2 tablespoons olive oil
	Salt and freshly ground pepper to taste
8 oz (250 g) fresh mushrooms	
3 cloves garlic, very finely chopped	3 oz (90 g) Gruyère cheese, freshly grated

In two pots of boiling salted water, cook the spaghetti and broccoli simultaneously for 8 minutes, or until both are *al dente*.

Meanwhile, sauté the mushrooms and garlic in the butter and oil.

Drain the spaghetti and broccoli in separate colanders, then toss together in a serving bowl, along with the mushrooms and their sautéing mixture, salt, pepper, and the Gruyère. Serve immediately.

Vermicelli Crown
with Mushroom Sauce

A luncheon dish, but a rather elegant one; it rather reminds me of moulded buffet dishes from the thirties. Though I don't know its provenance, I would guess that it is Scandinavian in origin.

8 oz (250 g) vermicelli
1 teaspoon butter
1 teaspoon plain flour
8 tablespoons milk
1 tablespoon double cream
1 egg, beaten

5 tablespoons freshly grated Parmesan cheese
Salt, freshly ground pepper, and nutmeg to taste
Mushroom Sauce (see below)

Preheat the oven to 350°F (175°C), mark 4.

Boil the vermicelli *al dente* (see page 26), then drain well.

Make a white sauce by melting the butter in a small saucepan, stirring in the flour, and adding the milk; simmer, stirring until thickened. Combine the cream and beaten egg and add a little sauce to it. Then, beating constantly, add the cream mixture to the hot sauce and heat carefully for a minute or two.

Fold the sauce into the drained vermicelli and pour into a greased ring mould. Place the mould in a roasting pan and fill the pan with boiling water to a point halfway up the side of the mould. Bake for 30 minutes, or until set.

Meanwhile, make the mushroom sauce. When the noodle ring is ready, turn the mould on to a serving dish. Pour the mushroom sauce into the centre of the ring and serve.

Mushroom Sauce

8 oz (250 g) fresh mushrooms,
    sliced
1 tablespoon very finely chopped
    shallots
8 tablespoons dry white wine,
    more if necessary
2 oz (60 g) butter, softened

1 oz (30 g) plain flour
1 tablespoon lemon juice
4 tablespoons double cream
1 egg yolk, beaten
Salt and freshly ground pepper
    to taste

Cook the mushrooms, shallots, and wine together for 10 minutes, then drain, reserving the wine.

Cream together the butter and flour. Add to the wine in a small saucepan and cook until thickened, adding more wine if the mixture is too thick. Add the lemon juice, cream, egg yolk, and mushrooms and cook, stirring, until thickened. Add salt and pepper to taste.

FISH AND SHELLFISH

FISH AND SHELLFISH

Prawns, Ricotta, and Vermicelli

Pink and white, prawns and ricotta go well with very thin noodles. This is a very quick dish, which can be assembled in 10 minutes – provided you have peeled prawns around.

8 oz (250 g) peeled prawns
2 tablespoons olive oil
1 teaspoon chopped fresh basil or ½ teaspoon dried
1 lb (500 g) vermicelli
1½ oz (45 g) butter, melted
8 oz (250 g) ricotta cheese*

Salt and freshly ground black pepper to taste
2 tablespoons chopped fresh parsley
2 oz (60 g) Parmesan cheese, freshly grated

In a small frying pan, sauté the prawns in the oil very briefly and toss with the basil. Set aside.

Boil the vermicelli *al dente* (see page 26), then drain well. Place in a warm bowl with 2 tablespoons of the melted butter.

Place the ricotta in a pan with the remaining tablespoon of butter and stir over a low heat until smooth and warm, then pour over the hot vermicelli. Top with the prawns, salt, pepper, parsley and grated cheese and toss. Serve immediately.

Mussels Leopardo

In the past mussels have been considered a 'poor' scavenger sort of dish, scarcely deserving of cookbook mention. Italian cooks have recognized their worth for a long time, however.

3 lb (1½ kg) mussels, well cleaned and debearded
8 tablespoons olive oil
3 cloves garlic, chopped
1 large tin (28 oz (875 g) size) Italian plum tomatoes, plus 1 small tin (8 oz (250 g) size) chopped well
½ teaspoon salt
1 bay leaf
½ teaspoon dried thyme
2 tablespoons finely chopped fresh parsley
Crushed dried red chillies* to taste
Freshly ground pepper to taste
8 tablespoons dry white wine or water
1 lb (500 g) vermicelli

Place the oil in a large pot. Add the garlic and sauté until browned, then add the tomatoes, salt, bay leaf, thyme, parsley, red chillies and black pepper, and simmer for 5 minutes. Add the wine or water, and bring to the boil. Add the mussels and cover the pot.

When all the mussels are open, set aside briefly, covered, while you boil the vermicelli *al dente* (see page 26). Drain the pasta, place in large soup bowls, and top with the mussel mixture. Serve with rounds of garlic toast.

Rigatoni with Squid

A hot, peppery squid sauce is a favourite in Italy. I like it best with large, firm noodles like rigatoni.

Squid should be cleaned under running water. Pull out the head and tentacles and the clear cartilage (which looks like a piece of plastic), then carefully pull off the purplish translucent skin.

4 tablespoons olive oil
1 lb (500 g) fresh squid, cleaned, skinned, and cut into wide pieces
2 cloves garlic, very finely chopped
1 green pepper, seeded and roughly chopped
3 fresh green chillies, seeded and finely chopped
Salt and red pepper flakes to taste
1 large tin (28 oz (875 g) size) Italian plum tomatoes, plus 1 small tin (8 oz (250 g) size), roughly chopped
1 tin (5 oz (160 g)) tomato paste
1 lb (500 g) rigatoni

Heat the oil in a heavy frying pan over a medium heat. Sauté the squid until curled, then add the garlic and lower the heat a little. Add the green pepper, chillies, salt, red pepper flakes, tomatoes, and tomato paste and simmer for 15 minutes. If the mixture is too thick, add water; if not thick enough, let simmer until thickened.

Cook the rigatoni *al dente*, then drain well, place in a serving bowl, and top with the sauce. Serve immediately.

Spaghetti with Sardines

An interesting combination of tastes – the bland, crunchy pine nuts with the two fishy tastes, as well as garlic, pasta, and raisins. This dish is traditionally served at Epiphany in Italy.

3 tablespoons olive oil
4 oz (125 g) pine nuts*
3 tins sardines, chopped
2 cloves garlic, very finely
  chopped
2 tins (2 oz (60 g) each) anchovies,
  mashed

2–3 oz (60–90 g) raisins (optional)
2 tablespoons chopped fresh
  parsley
1 lb (500 g) spaghetti

Heat the oil in a heavy frying pan and lightly brown the pine nuts in it. Add the sardines, garlic, and anchovies and sauté for 4 minutes, stirring well. Add the raisins, if used, and the parsley.

Boil the spaghetti *al dente* (see page 26), then drain and toss with the sardine mixture. Serve immediately.

Tagliatelle with Seafood Sauce

A wonderful one-dish meal that needs only a very plain salad and some crusty bread as an accompaniment.

8 tablespoons olive oil
1 small onion, very finely chopped
2 cloves garlic, very finely
  chopped

2 tablespoons very finely chopped
  fresh parsley
1 teaspoon salt

Freshly ground black pepper to taste

1 teaspoon finely chopped fresh thyme or ½ teaspoon dried

¾ pint (375 ml) double cream

8 tablespoons dry white wine

8 oz (250 g) medium prawns, peeled

8 oz (250 g) scallops

2 lb (1 kg) mussels, well scrubbed and debearded

1 lb (500 g) tagliatelle, freshly made (see pages 22–4) if possible

Heat the oil in a heavy frying pan. Add the onion and garlic and sauté until soft; do not let burn. Add the parsley, salt, pepper, thyme, cream, and wine and bring to the boil. Let boil for 5 to 8 minutes over a high heat, then reduce the heat to medium and add the prawns, scallops, and mussels. Cook, covered, until the mussels open.

Meanwhile, boil the tagliatelle *al dente* (see page 26), then drain and place in a large serving dish. Pour the sauce over, arranging the mussels on top. Serve immediately.

Spaghetti al Tonno

Italian pasta recipes often use tuna in extremely interesting ways. This recipe has a nice piquant flavour, due to the capers and anchovies. You could serve it with lemon wedges.

4 tablespoons olive oil

2 cloves garlic, very finely chopped

2 lb (1 kg) tomatoes, peeled, seeded, and chopped (see note on page 49)

1 tablespoon finely chopped fresh basil or 1 teaspoon dried

1 tin (7 oz (220 g)) tuna, drained and flaked

2 tablespoons capers

1 teaspoon very finely chopped anchovy or anchovy paste

Salt and freshly ground pepper to taste

1 lb (500 g) spaghetti

Heat the olive oil in a heavy saucepan, and sauté the garlic until lightly browned. Add the tomatoes and basil and simmer for 30 minutes, adding water if necessary. Add the tuna, capers, and anchovies, and salt and pepper to taste.

Boil the spaghetti *al dente* (see page 26), then drain, place in a serving bowl, and pour the sauce over. Serve immediately.

Vermicelli with Clam and Broccoli Sauce

Just as scallops and broccoli are complementary, so are clams and broccoli in a light garlicky sauce. Again, the warning to *undercook* the broccoli is important.

1 lb (500 g) fresh broccoli, washed and separated into florets
8 tablespoons olive oil
2 cloves garlic, peeled and sliced
2 tins (7 oz (220 g) each) clams,* the clams finely chopped and the juice reserved
½ teaspoon salt

Freshly ground black pepper to taste
½ teaspoon dried oregano
1 lb (500 g) vermicelli
2 tablespoons chopped fresh coriander or parsley
2 oz (60 g) Romano cheese,* freshly grated

Boil the broccoli for 4 or 5 minutes in a large saucepan of water, then taste; when you can just bite through the stem, the broccoli is done. Drain well and run cold water through it.

Heat the oil in a heavy frying pan and sauté the garlic for 2 minutes, stirring. Add the reserved clam juice, salt, pepper, and oregano. Add the clams and broccoli and cook, stirring, for a few minutes, until heated through.

Boil the vermicelli *al dente* (see page 26) and drain well. Stir the parsley or coriander into the sauce and toss with the vermicelli. Serve, sprinkled with the freshly grated Romano.

Simple White Clam Sauce

Clam sauce using tinned clams is very quick and a very good 'larder' meal, since you can keep the main ingredients on hand indefinitely.

2 tablespoons olive oil
4 cloves garlic, very finely chopped
2 tins (7 oz (220 g) size) clams,* juice of 1 tin reserved
8 tablespoons dry white wine
½ teaspoon dried thyme

6 tablespoons very finely chopped fresh parsley
12 oz (375 g) spaghetti
1 oz (30 g) butter
Salt and freshly ground pepper to taste

Heat the oil in a frying pan and sauté the garlic briefly, until golden. Add the clams, the reserved juice, and the wine and cook rapidly, to reduce the liquid, for 3 minutes. Lower the heat, add the thyme, parsley, salt, and pepper and set aside.

Boil the spaghetti *al dente* (see page 26) and toss first with the butter, then with the clam sauce. Serve at once.

Clams with Tomato Sauce and Spaghetti

Red clam sauce for pasta is excellent, and much more robust than the white variety – though my own opinion is that the heavy sauce rather tends to overwhelm the clams.

2 medium onions, very finely chopped
2 tablespoons olive oil
1 large tin (28 oz (875 g) size) Italian plum tomatoes, plus 1 small tin (8 oz (250 g) size)
1 tin (5 oz (160 g)) tomato paste
2 cloves garlic, pressed
1 tablespoon chopped fresh basil or 1 teaspoon dried

2 teaspoons granulated sugar
Salt and freshly ground black pepper to taste
2 tins (7 oz (220 g) each) clams,* juice reserved
3 oz (90 g) fresh mushrooms, sliced
1 lb (500 g) spaghetti
Freshly grated Parmesan cheese to taste

Sauté the onion in the oil until soft. Add the tomatoes and tomato paste, crushing the tomatoes with a spoon; then add the garlic, basil, sugar, salt, and pepper and let simmer briefly. Add the clams, with the reserved liquid, and the mushrooms. Boil the sauce down if too thin, then let simmer for at least 30 minutes.

Meanwhile, boil the spaghetti *al dente* (see page 26) and drain. Pour the sauce on individual servings of spaghetti and top with grated Parmesan.

Vermicelli with Tomato Sauce and Anchovies

A very simple anchovy sauce – another 'larder' dish, the ingredients of which you can have on hand for improvised suppers.

3 cloves garlic, chopped
3 tablespoons olive oil
2 tablespoons chopped chives
2 tins (2 oz (60 g) each) anchovy fillets, chopped
1 large tin (28 oz (875 g) size) Italian plum tomatoes, plus 1 small tin (8 oz (250 g) size)

1 tin (5 oz (160 g)) tomato paste
1 lb (500 g) vermicelli
Salt and freshly ground pepper to taste

Heat the oil in a frying pan and sauté the garlic until golden. Add the chives and the chopped anchovies and sauté briefly, stirring,

then add the tomatoes and the tomato paste, crushing the tomatoes with a wooden spoon. Add salt and pepper to taste and let the sauce simmer for at least 30 minutes.

Meanwhile, cook the vermicelli *al dente* (see page 26), then drain and toss with the tomato sauce. Serve immediately.

Spinach–Anchovy Cannelloni

Forgetting to bone the large anchovies I bought in an Italian market, I 'crunched' through my first trial of this dish. *Without* the bones, this is an excellent variation of the usual cheesy filling. Bought cannelloni are not as delicate as the freshly made variety, but they are very good and seem to suit the robust filling.

2 tablespoons olive oil

2 medium onions, finely chopped

3 cloves garlic, finely chopped

5 large anchovies, boned, or 1 tin 2 oz (60 g)) small anchovies, both chopped fine

1 oz (30 g) peperoni,* finely chopped

8 oz (250 g) fresh spinach, washed, drained, and picked over

Salt and freshly ground black pepper to taste

2 oz (60 g) Parmesan cheese, freshly grated

8 oz (250 g) cannelloni

8 oz (250 g) mozzarella,* roughly grated

Heat the oil in a large, heavy frying pan. Add the onion and garlic and sauté until golden, then add the anchovies and peperoni and sauté for 1 minute. Chop the spinach and place on top, cover, and cook, checking after 3 minutes to stir the spinach down. Cover again and cook until the spinach is wilted, then remove from the heat and add salt, pepper, and the Parmesan, and set aside.

Preheat the oven to 375°F (190°C), mark 5.

Boil the cannelloni in a large saucepan until just tender, then drain. Stuff each tube with 2 tablespoons of the filling mixture, then place the stuffed cannelloni on a buttered baking dish in one layer. Top with the grated mozzarella, then bake in the preheated oven until heated through, and until the cheese is bubbly on top.

Vermicelli with Mussel Sauce
à la Crème

The addition of cream to the simple mussel sauce makes this a very elegant dish.

2 lb (1 kg) mussels
1 lb (500 g) vermicelli
2 oz (60 g) butter
½ pint (250 ml) single cream
2 oz (60 g) Parmesan cheese, freshly grated

Salt and freshly ground black pepper to taste
2 tablespoons chopped fresh parsley

Clean and debeard the mussels, then steam them open in ½ inch (1 or 2 cm) water in a large saucepan, covered. Remove from the pan, but retain the liquid. Remove the mussels from their shells and pull off the sandy 'neck' skins. Chop roughly and set aside.

Boil the vermicelli *al dente* (see page 26) and drain well. Heat the butter in a heavy saucepan. Add the vermicelli and toss with the cream and Parmesan until hot. Add the mussels, the reserved mussel liquid, salt, and pepper, tossing. Serve immediately, with more Parmesan if desired and the parsley as a garnish.

Note: Tinned clams can be substituted for the mussels.

Escargots with Pasta

6 first-course servings

Snails in snail butter are here given a noodle treatment and the garlicky parsley butter is perfect for both. This is especially good for a first course, for which the following recipe is designed (the quantities have been adjusted to make smaller portions for six people).

12 oz (375 g) spaghettini or ordinary spaghetti
6 oz (190 g) butter

4 tablespoons very finely chopped spring onions
5 cloves garlic, mashed

Salt and freshly ground black
pepper to taste

2 small tins (7 oz (220 g) each)
snails, drained and roughly
chopped

6 tablespoons very finely chopped
fresh parsley

Boil the pasta *al dente* (see page 26).

Meanwhile, heat the butter in a small saucepan. When melted, add the spring onions, garlic, salt and pepper and sauté over a low heat for 3 minutes, stirring; do not allow the garlic to brown. Add the drained and chopped snails and toss, heating gently. Add the parsley.

Drain the pasta and place in a serving bowl. Pour the snail mixture over and toss, then serve at once. Serve freshly grated Parmesan cheese separately.

Plaki

Greek fish dishes are often very robust so it is best to use a fish that can stand up to the flavours of garlic, tomatoes, and salty olives. The coarser and firmer white fish are good; I often use cod.

4 tablespoons olive oil

4 medium onions, chopped

2 cloves garlic, very finely
chopped

3 stalks celery, chopped

5 tomatoes, peeled, seeded, and
sliced (see note on page 49)

Salt and freshly ground black
pepper to taste

12 oz (375 g) elbow macaroni

2 lb (1 kg) firm white fish fillets
(haddock, halibut, pollack, or
cod)

4 tablespoons lemon juice

8 black Greek olives, pitted and
chopped

4 tablespoons very finely chopped
fresh parsley

Preheat the oven to 350°F (175°C), mark 4.

Heat the oil in a frying pan and sauté the onion until golden. Add the garlic, celery, tomatoes, and salt and pepper and sauté over a low heat for 5 minutes.

Meanwhile, boil the macaroni *al dente* (see page 26). Drain, then place in a buttered casserole and put the sautéed vegetables on top. Place the fish on the vegetables, sprinkle with salt and pepper and lemon juice, and arrange the olives on top.

Bake, covered, for 30 minutes, or until the fish flakes easily with a fork. Garnish with the parsley and serve.

Scandinavian Fish Pudding

'Fish pudding' has a rather flat sound to it, but this creamy mixture is quite hearty and delicious. You might also want to add a tablespoon of capers.

4 oz (125 g) macaroni, cooked
1 oz (30 g) butter, melted
1 teaspoon salt
Freshly ground black pepper
1 lb (500 g) firm white fish (haddock, halibut, pollack, or cod), cooked and separated into chunks

8 tablespoons cream
8 tablespoons fish or clam stock
2 eggs, separated
3 oz (90 g) Gruyère cheese, freshly grated
1 tablespoon chopped fresh dill
1 oz (30 g) breadcrumbs

Preheat the oven to 350°F (175°C), mark 4.

Toss the macaroni with the salt, pepper, fish, butter, cream, stock, egg yolks, cheese, and dill. Beat the egg whites until stiff and pile on top of the macaroni mixture, then top with the breadcrumbs and bake for 40 minutes.

Chinese Mussel Sauce for Spaghetti or Fresh Chinese Noodles

Black beans and mussels make a wonderful sauce. It is also excellent with prawns, and is similar to the snail (periwinkle) sauce in this book (see page 124).

1 lb (500 g) spaghetti or fresh Chinese noodles*

3 tablespoons salted, fermented black beans*

1 tablespoon red wine vinegar

1 teaspoon granulated sugar

2 tablespoons soy sauce

2 tablespoons oyster sauce*

8 tablespoons chicken stock, clam stock, or water

3 fresh hot chillies, seeded and finely chopped

Rind of ½ lemon, cut into very thin strips

4 cloves garlic, very finely chopped

2 tablespoons chopped fresh ginger*

3 tablespoons groundnut oil

4 oz (125 g) minced pork

3 lb (1½ kg) mussels, scrubbed and debearded

1 tablespoon cornflour, dissolved in 4 tablespoons water

Boil the spaghetti or noodles *al dente* (see page 26), then drain well and keep warm.

Combine the black beans, vinegar, sugar, soy sauce, and oyster sauce. Add the stock or water and set aside.

Combine the chillies, lemon rind, garlic, and ginger and set aside.

Heat the oil in a wok. Add the pork and stir-fry until browned and separated, then add the chilli mixture and stir-fry for 2 minutes. Add the black bean mixture and stir-fry for 2 minutes more. Add the mussels, cover the wok, and cook until the mussels open.

Place the mussels in a large bowl, leaving the sauce in the wok.

Add the cornflour mixture, then bring the sauce to the boil, stirring. When thick, pour over the mussels and serve, along with the spaghetti or noodles.

Laksa

Laksa is a Malaysian dish that uses Chinese fishballs and a Malaysian version of curry powder; it is all held together by the omnipresent santan, or pressed coconut milk. You can make quite a bit of santan and freeze it for future use. (The amount of curry powder sounds like a lot; but somehow the Malaysian variety is not very hot; the heat is added by the chilli powder, which you should adjust to taste.)

2 lb (1 kg) thin noodles
12 oz (375 g) bean sprouts, washed and drained
2 tablespoons groundnut oil
1 teaspoon salt
6 tablespoons Malaysian curry powder, or 3 tablespoons Madras curry powder
3 teaspoons chilli powder, or to taste
1½ pints (750 ml) water
6 tablespoons tamarind* soaked in 8 tablespoons warm water
4 chicken bouillon cubes
¾ pint (375 ml) Santan (see below)
2 tins of packet Chinese fishballs (about 10),* drained

4–5 oz (125–160 g) peanuts, finely ground
2 cucumbers, peeled, cut in half lengthwise and seeded, then cut in thin strips
4 fresh chillies, seeded and cut into very thin shreds
3 squares bean curd,* pressed between two plates to remove excess liquid and cut into cubes
3 eggs, hard boiled
2 limes, cut in wedges
1 purple onion, cut into thin rings

Boil noodles *al dente* (see page 26). Drain well, then place in a serving bowl or in individual bowls.

Boil the bean sprouts for 1 minute in a large saucepan of boiling water, then drain well in a colander. Run cold water through them and set aside.

Heat the oil in a wok or heavy frying pan. Add the salt, curry powder, chilli powder, and 8 tablespoons of the water. Stir into a paste and fry for 2 minutes, stirring.

Drain the tamarind over a small bowl, squeezing to extract the liquid. Add the tamarind water to the paste and boil until reduced to a paste again.

Place the paste in a large saucepan. Add the rest of the water, the chicken bouillon cubes, the coconut liquid, and the fishballs. Heat through, just to boiling point, then add the ground peanuts.

Pour the 'soup' over the noodles, dividing the fishballs evenly, and serve. Accompany with a plate of the garnishes, or garnish each bowl separately with the following: cucumber strips, chilli shreds, hard-boiled egg (cut in quarters), lime wedges, onion rings, and bean curd cubes (deep-fried in groundnut oil until golden if desired).

Santan

Soak 3 oz (90 g) grated fresh coconut or unsweetened coconut shreds in 1¼ pints (625 ml) warm water for 15 minutes, then squeeze through a cloth into a bowl until you have ¾ pint (375 ml) liquid.

Pathai

This is a Thai noodle dish, one of a great tradition. The noodles to be used are cellophane or rice noodles. These come in swirls or twists in Thailand, but are also available in Chinese markets in small skeins.

Groundnut oil as needed
5 oz (160 g) raw, skinned, peanuts
3 heads garlic, separated into cloves, then peeled and sliced
4 oz (125 g) pork tenderloin, shredded
8 oz (250 g) prawns, peeled
2 squares bean curd,* cut into cubes
1 lb (500 g) cellophane noodles,* soaked in warm water and drained
1 oz (30 g) dried shrimp,* soaked in warm water
2 tablespoons fish sauce*
1 tablespoon vinegar
1 teaspoon granulated sugar
2 eggs, lightly beaten
Lime wedges for garnish

Brush a heavy frying pan with groundnut oil and place the peanuts in it over a medium heat, shaking the pan occasionally to brown the peanuts evenly. Set the peanuts aside.

Add 2 or 3 tablespoons of oil to the pan and fry the garlic until brown and crisp – but *do not let it burn*. Remove with a slotted spoon and drain on paper towels. Add the pork strips to the pan and cook, stirring, until brown.

Add the prawns, the bean curd, and the noodles, then add ¼ pint (125 ml) or so of water and cover to steam the noodles for about a minute. Add the dried shrimp, drained, and the fish sauce, vinegar, and sugar. Add the garlic bits.

Scramble the eggs in a small frying pan, then cut them into bits and add to the pan. Arrange all the ingredients on a serving dish and garnish with the peanuts. Serve with lime wedges.

Unagi Donburi

Unagi donburi, or grilled eel on a bowl of rice – a very common and delicious Japanese dish – loses nothing in its translation into a noodle dish. The sauce, slurped up with soba noodles, is lovely when the eel or fish juices have dripped into it.

12 oz (375 g) mackerel or eel, cleaned, boned, and filleted	1 teaspoon aonoriko (dried, pulverized seaweed)* (optional)
¼ pint (125 ml) soy sauce	1 lb (500 g) thin soba noodles*
2 tablespoons plus 1 teaspoon sesame oil*	2 tablespoons rice wine vinegar*
	2 spring onions, finely chopped
2½ teaspoons granulated sugar	

Marinate the fish with 2 tablespoons of the soy sauce, 1 teaspoon of the sesame oil, and ½ teaspoon of the sugar for 30 minutes, then sprinkle with aonoriko (optional) and grill for 10 minutes, or until done.

Meanwhile, boil the noodles *al dente* (see page 26) and drain them; combine the rest of the soy sauce, 2 tablespoons sesame oil, 2 teaspoons sugar, and 2 tablespoons vinegar and set aside.

Divide noodles among individual serving bowls. Cut the fish into bowl-sized segments and place on top. Garnish with the spring onions.

Each diner pours sauce over his own fish and noodles.

Chinese Periwinkles with Spaghetti

This is my favourite of all snail recipes, Chinese or otherwise. We go on expeditions every summer to get them from a restaurant that has made its reputation (for us, at least) on this dish alone. The slight fuss in eating them, picking them out of the shell and discarding the hard, flat disc off the end before eating, is well worth it, and gives the meal a pleasant leisurely quality.

1 tablespoon granulated sugar
1 teaspoon salt
1 tablespoon cornflour
2 tablespoons salted, fermented black beans,* washed and mashed with a fork
2 tablespoons soy sauce
2 tablespoons hoisin sauce*
½ teaspoon crushed dried red chillies,* or to taste
2–3 lb (1–1½ kg) periwinkles
3 tablespoons groundnut oil

2 teaspoons sesame oil*
1½ tablespoons finely chopped, fresh ginger*
2 cloves garlic, very finely chopped
5 spring onions, finely chopped
3 fresh green chillies, shredded
4 tablespoons dry sherry
½ pint (250 ml) chicken stock
1 lb (500 g) spaghetti or fresh Chinese noodles*

Combine the sugar, salt, cornflour, mashed black beans, soy sauce, hoisin sauce, and dried red peppers. Set aside.

Soak the periwinkles in cold water for an hour, scrubbing them by rubbing them together under water, and changing the water often. Smell them one by one for freshness.

Heat a wok. Add the groundnut and sesame oils, then the ginger, garlic, spring onions, and fresh chillies. Add the sherry and simmer for 1 minute, then add the periwinkles, and stir-fry for 2 minutes. Add the reserved seasoning mixture and the stock and bring to a simmer, stirring. Let simmer for 5 minutes.

Boil the spaghetti or noodles *al dente* (see page 26), then drain well and place in a large bowl. Serve with the periwinkles and sauce poured over.

Note: Provide long hat pins for getting the periwinkles out of their shells.

Soba Noodles with Tempura

In Japan, *tempura soba* is quite popular as a lunch or evening snack, and the most popular tempura is prawn. Serve tempura as quickly as possible after frying it. It should be eaten off the top of the noodles and not dunked, as it becomes soggy quickly.

1 egg yolk
8 fl oz (200 ml) iced water
Generous 4 oz (125 g) plain flour
½ pint (250 ml) chicken stock
1 tablespoon finely chopped fresh ginger*
2 tablespoons dry sherry
2 tablespoons soy sauce
Vegetable oil for deep frying
6 large fresh mushrooms

1 green pepper, seeded and cut into strips
8 oz (250 g) prawns, peeled
1 lb (500 g) soba noodles* boiled *al dente* (see page 26) and drained
4 tablespoons grated fresh daikon (long white horseradish)*
1 tablespoon granulated sugar

To prepare a batter, first place the egg yolk in a bowl. Beat it well, adding the iced water while beating, then the flour all at once. Beat only briefly after the flour is added, as the batter should be lumpy. Set aside.

Heat together, in a small saucepan, the chicken stock, sugar, sherry, and soy sauce. Heat just until the sugar dissolves, then set aside.

Heat the oil in a deep frying pan or wok. Let one drop of tempura batter drip in; if it rises quickly and browns lightly in less than a minute, the oil is hot enough. Dip the vegetables and prawns in the batter and fry, a few at a time, until golden. Drain on paper towels.

While the fried foods are draining, divide the noodles between 6 individual bowls. Add the grated daikon and ginger and pour the hot sauce over each. Place an assortment of tempura on each bowl and serve.

Prawn Patia with Vermicelli

Prawn patia is an Indian dish I first had in London, and I have been searching for that taste ever since. I have here put together several versions of it in an approximation of my first experience. Use fewer chillies if you want to make the dish less hot.

½ teaspoon salt
1 teaspoon ground cumin
½ teaspoon crushed hot red pepper
3 tablespoons corn oil
1 tablespoon groundnut oil
2 large onions, sliced
1 green pepper, finely chopped
1 teaspoon finely chopped fresh ginger*
3 cloves garlic, finely chopped
4 fresh green chillies, finely chopped

1 lb (500 g) prawns, peeled combined with ½ teaspoon ground turmeric
1 14 oz (440 g) tin Italian plum tomatoes, roughly chopped
4 tablespoons water
1 lb (500 g) vermicelli
Chopped fresh coriander for garnish

Heat a heavy frying pan. Stir the salt, cumin, and red pepper in it over a high heat for 1 minute, then lower the heat, add the oils, the onion and the green pepper and stir for 5 minutes, until the onion is wilted.

Add the ginger, garlic, and chillies and stir for another minute, then add the prawns. Add the tomatoes and the water and stir. Let simmer until the mixture is fairly thick.

Boil the vermicelli *al dente* (see page 26) and drain well. Serve with the prawn mixture poured over, and garnished with the chopped coriander.

Peking Noodles with Prawns

Peking noodles usually denotes a dish of flat noodles with a very pungent pork sauce. Here, however, the same sauce lightened a bit does very well with prawns.

5 dried mushrooms,* soaked in water for 30 minutes, soaking liquid reserved

2 tablespoons plus 2 teaspoons sesame oil*

3 tablespoons hoisin sauce*

2 tablespoons soy sauce*

1 clove garlic, very finely chopped

2 tablespoons groundnut oil

8 oz (250 g) prawns, peeled

1 teaspoon sherry or liquid from the dried mushrooms

1 lb (500 g) fresh Chinese noodles* or spaghetti

6 spring onions, green part and white, cleaned and chopped

Slice the mushrooms into thin strips, then set aside in the soaking liquid.

Combine the 2 teaspoons sesame oil, the hoisin sauce, the soy sauce, and the garlic. Set aside.

Heat the groundnut oil in a wok or heavy frying pan over a high flame. Add the prawns and stir-fry very briefly. Drain the mushrooms, reserving the soaking liquid, and add to the wok, then add the reserved sesame oil–hoisin sauce mixture, and 1 teaspoon sherry or mushroom liquid. Cook over a reduced heat for about 2 minutes and set aside.

In a large saucepan of boiling water, cook the noodles for 5 minutes if fresh or until tender if dried. Drain well and toss with the 2 tablespoons sesame oil in a serving bowl. Toss with the prawn mixture, garnish with the chopped spring onions, and serve immediately.

Chinese Browned Noodles with Prawns

I like the taste of double-cooked noodles: first boiled, then fried in a little oil to brown around the edges, a favourite Chinese method that would translate well to other kinds of noodles.

5 dried mushrooms*
½ pint (250 ml) boiling water
4 oz (125 g) fresh mushrooms, sliced
7 tablespoons corn or peanut oil
8 oz (250 g) prawns, peeled
Salt to taste
2 tablespoons cornflour

1 tablespoon soy sauce
1 teaspoon granulated sugar
8–12 oz (250–375 g) fresh Chinese noodles* or spaghetti
8 tablespoons chopped spring onion green
½ pint (250 ml) chicken stock or mushroom liquid

Soak dried mushrooms in the boiling water for 15 to 30 minutes. Squeeze dry, reserving the soaking liquid.

Sauté the fresh mushrooms in 2 tablespoons of the oil until browned, then set aside.

Combine the 2 tablespoons cornflour, soy sauce, and sugar and set aside.

Boil the noodles for 4 or 5 minutes. Drain immediately in a colander, then run cold water through the noodles until cool. Set aside.

Split the prawns by slicing almost through ('butterflying'), then toss with sesame oil and the fresh and dried mushrooms and spring onion green and set aside.

Heat the remaining 3 tablespoons oil in the wok. Add the noodles and flatten into a 'pancake' over a very high heat. Press down with a spatula as it browns and turn once to brown the other side.

Heat the prawn mixture in a frying pan over a high flame, adding the stock or mushroom liquid mixed with the reserved cornflour mixture. Stir well.

Place the noodles on a serving dish, top with the prawn mixture, and serve immediately.

Mee Krob (Thai Rice Stick with Pork and Prawns)

This Thai dish has many interesting contrasts – the crisp, lightly fried noodles and rich smooth sauce, the nearly cloying hoisin sauce 'cut' by lemon peel, the contrasting textures of fresh bean sprouts, pork, and prawns. This is an impressive dish to serve.

Corn oil for deep frying, mixed with 1 tablespoon sesame oil*

2 eggs, beaten with $\frac{1}{4}$ teaspoon cayenne pepper and $\frac{1}{2}$ teaspoon salt

12 oz (375 g) rice stick noodles,* pulled apart into 3- or 4-inch (7–10 cm) one-layered sections

2 tablespoons groundnut oil

2 onions, finely chopped

3 cloves garlic, finely chopped

1 lb (500 g) pork tenderloin, sliced into paper-thin pieces 2 inches (5 cm) long

8 oz (250 g) prawns, peeled

4 tablespoons hoisin sauce*

2 tablespoons tomato paste

$1\frac{1}{2}$ oz (45 g) granulated sugar

3 tablespoons fish sauce*

1 tablespoon slivered lemon peel

Juice of 1 lemon

8 oz (250 g) fresh bean sprouts, washed and drained

3 fresh green chillies, sliced very thin

8 spring onions, cut into 4-inch (10-cm) sections, both ends fringed by cutting through with a sharp knife and placed in iced water to curl

Heat the corn and sesame oils in a large frying pan or wok to 325°F (160°C) on a deep-frying thermometer. Let the egg fall through a slotted spoon to form lacy pancakes on the surface of the oil. Fry until brown, then turn and brown other side. (The total cooking time will be less than 1 minute.) Drain on paper towels. Repeat until egg is used up.

Raise the heat to 375°F (190°C). Drop in one piece of rice stick at a time; it will swell and brown. Turn and brown the other side, then drain on paper towels. Repeat with the remaining rice sticks. Remove the oil and clean out the wok.

Add the groundnut oil to the wok and heat. Add the onion, garlic, prawns, pork, hoisin sauce, tomato paste, sugar and fish sauce and cook until thick, about 20 minutes, over a medium heat. Add the lemon peel and juice.

Toss the prawn mixture with half the rice stick noodles and place in a large serving bowl. Pile the rest of the noodles on top in a conical mound, spread the egg 'lace' around the sides, and arrange the bean sprouts as a 'fringe'. Scatter the chilli shreds over all and garnish with the curled spring onions, arranged like spokes around the cone.

Note: If you do not have a thermometer test the oil with a noodle or a small cube of bread. If it browns in 60 seconds, it is hot enough. If the oil smokes it is too hot.

Noodles with Scallops, Broccoli, and Mushrooms

Scallops and broccoli contrast interestingly in colour, texture, and taste if you are careful not to overcook the broccoli. Serve with soy sauce if you like, but this is actually unnecessary, for the simple contrasts should be preserved without the binding and masking functions of a strong sauce.

1 head broccoli, separated into florets
2 tablespoons groundnut oil
1 tablespoon finely chopped fresh ginger*
1 teaspoon finely chopped garlic
8 oz (250 g) scallops, cut up if large

6 dried mushrooms,* soaked in warm water for 20 minutes, squeezed dry, and sliced
1 teaspoon salt
1 lb (500 g) fresh Chinese noodles* or spaghetti

Cook the broccoli until barely tender, then drain well and set aside.

Heat the oil in a heavy frying pan or wok and add the ginger and garlic. Stir-fry until golden, then add the scallops and stir-fry for 2 minutes. Add the broccoli, mushrooms, and salt and stir-fry quickly for 2 minutes longer.

Boil the noodles *al dente* (see page 26). Drain well and let dry a few minutes, spread out on a large dish, then add to the wok and brown over a high heat, tossing with the scallop mixture. Serve at once, with soy sauce, if desired.

Kung Pao Squid with Spaghetti

Kung Pao is a style of Chinese cooking, hot and garlicky and rich with bean paste, which is often used with prawns. We are adapting this for use with squid, which is a delicious substitute.

2 lb (1 kg) squid
2 tablespoons rice wine vinegar*
Salt to taste
1 teaspoon chilli paste with garlic*
1 tablespoon hoisin sauce*
1 tablespoon crushed yellow
    beans*
2 tablespoons soy sauce
4 teaspoons granulated sugar

4 cloves garlic, very finely
    chopped
2 tablespoons chopped spring
    onions
2 tablespoons finely chopped fresh
    ginger*
2 tablespoons groundnut oil
1 lb (500 g) fresh Chinese
    noodles* or spaghetti

Clean the squid by pulling out the 'head' and insides. Remove the hard cartilage, then carefully peel off the very thin purple skin. Cut into 2-inch (5-cm) squares, rinse, and pat dry.

In a mixing bowl, combine the vinegar, salt, chilli paste, hoisin sauce, crushed yellow beans, soy sauce, and sugar. In another bowl, combine the garlic, spring onions and ginger.

Heat the oil in a wok. Add the squid and stir-fry until curled and white. Add the ginger-garlic-spring onion mixture and stir-fry for 2 minutes, then add the vinegar mixture and stir until it simmers.

Meanwhile, boil the noodles *al dente* (see page 26) and drain well. Pour the squid sauce over the noodles and serve immediately.

Khanom Jeen Nam Prik

This Thai dish uses whatever seafood is seasonal and fresh. It is a 'wet' noodle dish, and should be served in large soup bowls.

5 cloves garlic, chopped
2 tablespoons groundnut oil
8 oz (250 g) pork, thinly sliced
¾ pint (375 ml) chicken or clam stock
2 tablespoons light soy sauce
3 dried red chillies,* pounded
8 oz (250 g) prawns, peeled
1 tablespoon sesame oil*
1 lb (500 g) thin egg noodles

12 freshly scrubbed and de-bearded mussels
1 tablespoon lemon juice
1 bunch spring onions, chopped (about 8 tablespoons)
4 oz (125 g) fresh bean sprouts
1½ oz (45 g) dry-roasted peanuts, chopped (peanuts roasted without oil – if not available use ordinary roasted nuts)

Heat the groundnut oil in a saucepan and sauté the garlic briefly. Add the pork and stir-fry briefly, until it changes colour. Add the stock and soy sauce, then bring to the boil and add the chillies, prawns, and sesame oil.

Meanwhile, boil the noodles *al dente* (see page 26), then drain and place in a serving bowl. Keep warm.

Add the mussels to the mixture in the saucepan and simmer, covered, until their shells open. Add the lemon juice and spring onions and remove from the heat. Stir in the bean sprouts and pour over the noodles. Garnish with the roasted peanuts and serve immediately.

Burmese Noodles with Prawn Tok
(Minced Prawns and Spicy Salad)

This prawn *tok* is served over a 'pickled' vegetable salad. The method of preparing prawns is very interesting. You could use these strips in a clear soup with seaweed as a Japanese-style Burmese soup.

12 oz (375 g) prawns, peeled and
  put through a meat mincer
3 tablespoons sesame oil*
3 tablespoons groundnut oil
1 medium cucumber, shredded
  and seeded
8 oz (250 g) Chinese cabbage,*
  shredded
1 carrot, scraped and shredded
3 spring onions, shredded

2 tablespoons soy sauce
Salt and freshly ground black
  pepper to taste
1 teaspoon very finely chopped
  fresh ginger*
½ teaspoon crushed dried red
  chillies*
1 lb (500 g) thin egg noodles
Chopped fresh green chillies for
  garnish

Shape the prawn meat into flat patties. Combine 1 tablespoon of
the sesame oil and the groundnut oil and heat in a wok. Fry the
patties over very high heat until browned and heated through. Drain
on paper towels, then, when cooled, slice into ½-inch (1-cm) slices.

Combine the cucumber, cabbage, carrot, spring onions, soy sauce,
salt and pepper, 1 tablespoon of the sesame oil, ginger, and dried red
chillies to make a salad. Set aside.

Boil the egg noodles *al dente* (see page 26), then drain well and
toss with the remaining sesame oil. Set aside to cool to room temperature, tossing occasionally, then place on a serving dish and
spread the salad on top. Arrange the prawn-patty shreds on top of
the salad, then serve, garnished with the chopped green chillies.

MEATS

Aubergine-Meat Casserole
with Macaroni

Aubergine and minced beef combine well here, and in dishes like
moussaka. The addition of hard-boiled egg is true to southern
Italian tradition.

Salt

1 medium aubergine, peeled and
  sliced

8 oz (250 g) macaroni

6 tablespoons olive oil, or as
  needed

Freshly ground black pepper to
  taste

1 lb (500 g) lean minced beef

2 hard-boiled eggs, diced

8 oz (250 g) mozzarella,* thinly
  sliced

2 oz (60 g) Parmesan cheese,
  freshly grated

1 oz (30 g) butter

Preheat the over to 350°F (175°C), mark 4.

Salt the aubergine slices and place in a colander to drain for 30
minutes. Pat dry with paper towels.

Boil the macaroni *al dente* (see page 26) and drain well.

Heat the olive oil in a frying pan. Brown the aubergine a few
slices at a time, and toss with salt and pepper. Add more oil as
needed. Remove the aubergine to another dish.

Add the beef to the frying pan and sauté, stirring, until broken up
and browned. Off the heat, stir in the egg and more salt and pepper.

In a buttered casserole, layer the macaroni, aubergine, meat, and
mozzarella, ending with a layer of aubergine. Top with the Parmesan, dot with the butter, and bake for 40 minutes.

Lentil Beef with Pasta

This is a good, hearty dish, rather like the lentil version of *pasta e fagioli*, but richer for the addition of meat. And, like all stews, best made a day ahead (except, of course, for the macaroni).

2 tablespoons olive oil
2 lb (1 kg) chuck steak, cut into 1-inch (2- or 3-cm) cubes
4 onions, finely chopped
2 cloves garlic, very finely chopped
1¼ pints (625 ml) beef stock

Salt and freshly ground black pepper to taste
½ teaspoon dried oregano
½ teaspoon dried basil
6 oz (190 g) red lentils, soaked in water for 2 hours
8 oz (250 g) macaroni

Heat the oil in a heavy casserole. Brown the beef and onion in it, then add the garlic, stock, salt and pepper, oregano, and basil. Partially cover and cook for 45 minutes to an hour.

Add the lentils, drained, and cook for 30 minutes more, or until the beef and lentils are tender.

Meanwhile, cook the macaroni *al dente* (see page 26) and drain well. Place the macaroni in a serving bowl and pour the meat and lentils over it.

Red, White, and Green Pasta

This is an attractive, Italian-flag-coloured dish, with a spicy, smoky taste from the bacon and peperoni. Full of spirit.

1 lb (500 g) farfalle or gemelli
6 rashers bacon, cut into 1-inch (2- or 3-cm) pieces
4 slices peperoni,* shredded
6 oz (190 g) fresh mushrooms, sliced

3 tomatoes, peeled, seeded, and chopped (see note on page 49)
1 large spring onion, chopped
Salt and freshly ground black pepper to taste

Cook the pasta *al dente* (see page 26) and drain well.

Sauté the bacon until crisp in a heavy frying pan. Pour out all but 2 tablespoons of the fat, then add the peperoni and sauté briefly.

Add the mushrooms and sauté, stirring, for 5 minutes, or until wilted; add the tomatoes and simmer just until soft. Season with salt and pepper and toss with the pasta and spring onion, then serve, offering freshly grated Parmesan cheese separately.

Prosciutto and Tomatoes
with Vermicelli

Prosciutto (ham) deserves the centre of the stage once in a while, and when it gets it, as in this recipe, it should be good, imported prosciutto. You can cheat elsewhere.

1 oz (30 g) butter	½ pint (250 ml) chicken stock
6 oz (190 g) prosciutto, cut into thin slivers	Salt and freshly ground black pepper to taste
4 medium tomatoes, peeled, seeded, and chopped (see note on page 49)	1 lb (500 g) vermicelli
	2 tablespoons chopped chives

Heat the butter in a saucepan and sauté the ham over a low heat. Add the tomatoes, chicken stock, and salt and pepper and simmer for about 15 minutes, allowing the liquid to reduce a little.

Boil the vermicelli *al dente* (see page 26) and drain well. Toss with the sauce, garnish with the chives, and serve.

Rotini with Sausages,
Peperoni, and Navy Beans

This is your basic beans and sausages, enlivened by a spicy and rich tomato sauce and served over whatever interesting pasta you like. Rotini or penne would be good here.

2 tablespoons olive oil	1 large fresh green chilli, finely chopped
2 onions, finely chopped	
2 cloves garlic, finely chopped	

1 lb (500 g) fresh Italian pork
  sausages,* sliced
1 peperoni,* thinly sliced
1 large tin (28 oz (875 g) size)
  Italian plum tomatoes, plus 1
  small tin (8 oz (250 g) size),
  roughly chopped
1½ tins (14 oz (440 g) size) cannellini (white kidney beans),
  drained and rinsed

1 tablespoon chopped fresh basil
  or 1 teaspoon dried
1 teaspoon granulated sugar
Salt and freshly ground black
  pepper to taste
2 oz (60 g) Parmesan cheese,
  freshly grated
1 lb (500 g) rotini

Preheat the oven to 350°F (175°C), mark 4.

Sauté the onion in the oil until golden. Add the garlic and fresh chilli and sauté for 5 minutes, then add the pork sausages and peperoni and sauté for 5 minutes longer. Add the tomatoes, beans, and seasonings.

Boil the rotini *al dente* (see page 26). Drain well and toss with the sauce, then place in a casserole and top with the grated cheese. Bake for 45 minutes.

Lasagne

This dish can be assembled as much as a day ahead and baked at the last minute. It is important, however, to bring the lasagne to room temperature before baking to be sure it cooks through.

1¾ pints (1 litre) tomato purée
1 5 oz (160 g) tin tomato paste
½ pint (250 ml) water
1 teaspoon dried oregano
1 teaspoon granulated sugar
½ tablespoon olive oil
2 large onions, chopped
1 clove garlic, very finely chopped

1 lb (500 g) minced beef
Salt
1 lb (500 g) lasagne, green is
  preferable
1 lb (500 g) mozzarella, sliced thin
1 lb (500 g) ricotta cheese
4 oz (125 g) Parmesan or Romano
  cheese,* grated

Combine the tomato purée, tomato paste, water, oregano, and sugar in a large saucepan and simmer over low heat. Meanwhile, sauté the onion and garlic in a heavy frying pan until golden, then add the beef and salt to taste and cook, stirring, until the beef is browned and separated. Add to the tomatoes.

Cook the lasagne in a large saucepan of boiling water, stirring to see that it does not stick. As it comes to the *al dente* stage, drain in a colander, run cold water over it, and toss in a large pot with oil, to keep it from sticking.

Grease a large casserole or baking tin and layer the lasagne, tomato sauce, ricotta, and mozzarella, with Parmesan sprinkled on every other layer, and finishing with ricotta and Parmesan. Bake at 375°F (190°C), mark 5 for 30 minutes.

Note: This can be covered with foil and stored in the refrigerator before baking.

Green and White Noodles with Ham and Mushrooms

Like other tagliatelle and ham combinations, this dish depends for its success on freshly made pasta (bought or homemade), good ham, and last minute assemblage.

1 lb (500g) fresh mushrooms, chopped

3 spring onions or two shallots, finely chopped

3 oz (90 g) butter

Salt and freshly ground pepper to taste

6 oz (190 g) ham, cut into thin strips

½ pint (250 ml) double cream

8 oz (250 g) each fresh green spinach noodles, and fresh white noodles, either home-made (see pages 22–4) or shop-bought

2 oz (60 g) Romano cheese,★ freshly grated

Fresh parsley for garnish

Heat half the butter in a heavy frying pan. Add the spring onions and mushrooms and stir over a medium heat until the mushrooms give off their juices. Add salt and pepper to taste, then turn down the heat and add the ham. Set aside.

Boil two pots of water, one for each kind of pasta. Cook *al dente* (see page 26) and drain well.

Meanwhile, place the remaining butter in a heatproof serving dish and warm it in a low oven. Put the pasta in the dish, then toss with the cream. Add the ham and mushroom mixture. Top with the Romano, garnish with parsley, and serve immediately.

Spaghetti Carbonara

Carbonara is an Italian classic. It is delicious, and extremely quick and easy to prepare. Some recipes have you leave all the bacon fat in; I remove most of it.

1 tablespoon olive oil	2 eggs
1 medium onion, very finely chopped	2 tablespoons freshly grated Romano pecorino cheese*
12 oz (375 g) bacon, very finely chopped	Salt and freshly ground black pepper to taste
1 lb (500 g) spaghetti	Snipped chives for garnish

Heat the oil in a frying pan and sauté the onion until golden. Add the bacon and sauté until just done, not crisp. Drain off all but 2 tablespoons of the fat.

Meanwhile, bring a large saucepan of water to the boil and start cooking the spaghetti. While the spaghetti is cooking, beat the eggs and cheese together. Set aside. Drain the spaghetti and put in a serving dish.

Add salt and pepper to the bacon mixture and stir. (If there is more than ¾ tablespoon of oil and fat in the frying pan, drain some off.) Add the egg mixture to the frying pan and stir well, adding salt if needed. Toss with the spaghetti, garnish with the chives, and serve at once.

Pasta with Beans and Sausage

This is one of the first dishes I ever made as an adult (I don't count childhood fudge making), and it goes through transformations constantly. Different sorts of beans, sausages, and shapes of pasta appear in it, rarely ones that don't go quite well with each other. If there is time, I use dried beans cooked *al dente*. Tinned beans are often mushy.

2 medium onions

8 oz (250 g) chorizo,* or other sausage

1½ tins (14 oz (440 g) size) cannellini (white kidney beans)

2 lb (1 kg) tomatoes

2 cloves garlic, diced or pressed

1 tablespoon chopped fresh basil or 1 teaspoon dried

½ teaspoon granulated sugar

Salt and freshly ground black pepper to taste

1 lb (500 g) egg noodles

1 oz (30 g) butter

2 oz (60 g) Parmesan cheese, freshly grated

Sauté the onion and sausage in a casserole, then add the tomatoes, beans, garlic, basil, and seasonings and mix well. Cook over a low heat for at least 40 minutes.

Boil the egg noodles *al dente* (see page 26), then drain and toss with the butter and cheese. Pour the sauce over and serve.

Spaghetti with Hot Italian Sausages and Basil Meatballs

Allowing myself only one Italian meatball and spaghetti recipe, I chose this one – a nearly perfect version of the dish. The meatballs, sausages, and sauce are also good baked in layers with lasagne pasta.

Meatballs

1 medium onion, finely chopped

2 cloves garlic, finely chopped

2 tablespoons olive oil

2 tablespoons freshly grated Parmesan or Romano* cheese

1½ lb (750 g) minced beef and pork, mixed

3 slices white bread, soaked in 8

tablespoons milk and squeezed dry

2 eggs

Salt and freshly ground black pepper

2 tablespoons finely chopped fresh basil or 1 tablespoon dried

Sauce

- 1 onion, finely chopped
- 2 cloves garlic, very finely chopped
- 2 tablespoons olive oil
- 1 tin (14 oz (440 g)) Italian plum tomatoes, blended until smooth
- 1 large tin (28 oz (875 g) size) Italian plum tomatoes, plus 1 small tin (8 oz (250 g) size)
- 2 tins (5 oz (160 g)) tomato paste
- 1 tablespoon granulated sugar
- Salt and freshly ground pepper to taste
- 1 tablespoon finely chopped fresh basil or 1½ teaspoons dried
- 1½ lb (750 g) hot Italian sausages,* cut into 1-inch (2- or 3-cm) chunks, sautéed until brown, and well drained
- 2 lb (1 kg) spaghetti

Make the meatballs first. Sauté the onion and garlic in the oil until golden, then combine with all the other meatball ingredients. Knead the mixture until it is smooth and well blended, then make walnut-sized meatballs and chill them on a large dish for 30 minutes.

Meanwhile, make the sauce. Sauté the onion and garlic together in the oil in a heavy frying pan. When golden, add all the other sauce ingredients except the sausages and simmer over a very low heat for 30 minutes.

Sauté the meatballs, a few at a time, in a large frying pan. As they brown and become firm, add them to the tomato sauce. Pour off the accumulated fat from the frying pan, then sauté the sausages. Add them to the sauce and let simmer for 30 minutes. Serve on the hot spaghetti, boiled *al dente* (see page 26).

Vermicelli with Meat Sauce and Feta Cheese

Feta, with its dry sharpness, is an excellent foil to a hearty meat sauce. Serve right after you add the feta to the sauce; you should be eating it as it begins to melt in.

1 medium onion, chopped
2 tablespoons olive oil
12 oz (375 g) minced beef
1 large tin (28 oz (875 g) size) Italian plum tomatoes, plus 1 small tin (8 oz (250 g) size)
1 tin (5 oz (160 g)) tomato paste
Salt and freshly ground black pepper to taste

1 tablespoon granulated sugar
4 tablespoons chopped fresh basil or 2 tablespoons dried
6 oz (190 g) feta cheese
1 lb (500 g) vermicelli
½ oz (15 g) butter

Sauté the onion in the olive oil over a medium heat, then add the minced beef and sauté until the meat is browned and broken up. Add the tomatoes and tomato paste. Mix well, then add the salt, pepper, sugar, and basil and let simmer. Add the cheese to the sauce just before serving.

Meanwhile, boil the vermicelli *al dente* (see page 26), then drain and mix with the butter in a serving bowl. Serve, topped with the sauce.

Pasta with Minced Beef
Cooked in Wine

This beef sauce from Lombardy is aromatic with fennel. It must be reheated the next day to take full advantage of the seasonings.

1 oz (30 g) butter
2 onions, finely chopped
1½ lb (750 g) minced beef
Salt and freshly ground black pepper to taste
Pinch of freshly grated nutmeg
3 bay leaves
1 chicken or beef bouillon cube

1 large tin (28 oz (875 g) size) Italian plum tomatoes, plus 1 small tin (8 oz (250 g) size)
6 fl oz (190 ml) dry red wine
1½ tablespoons fennel seeds, tied in cheesecloth
1 lb (500 g) spaghetti

Heat the butter in a frying pan and sauté the onion until golden. Add the beef and stir until browned and broken up, then add the remaining ingredients (except the spaghetti) and simmer for 30 to 45 minutes (in Italy it is left to cook at the back of the stove overnight). Remove the bag of fennel seeds, then refrigerate until serving time.

Boil the spaghetti *al dente* (see page 26), then drain well and serve with the sauce, reheated, and freshly grated Parmesan cheese.

Bahmie Goreng (Indonesian
Fried Noodles)

These fried noodles contain a number of fascinations of mine, including fish sauce and dried mushrooms. The way the pork is treated in this dish is particularly appealing, and the final assemblage is an orgy of tastes.

4 large dried mushrooms,* soaked in boiling water for 15 minutes, soaking liquid reserved

1 tablespoon dark soy sauce*
1 teaspoon molasses

12 oz (375 g) boneless pork tenderloin
1 lb (500 g) fresh Chinese
noodles* or spaghetti
4 tablespoons groundnut oil
1 large onion, cut into thin slivers
4 oz (125 g) Chinese cabbage,*
shredded

1 clove garlic, very finely chopped
2 fresh green chillies, seeded and
very finely chopped
8 oz (250 g) prawns, peeled
1 teaspoon fish sauce,* or to taste
2 tablespoons light soy sauce*
Chopped spring onions for garnish

Squeeze the mushrooms dry and slice, reserving the soaking liquid.

Combine the dark soy sauce and molasses in a glass or ceramic bowl and marinate the pork for 1 hour, then roast the pork in a small pan, with the marinade, for 45 minutes in a moderate oven. Cool and cut in strips.

Boil the noodles *al dente* (see page 26), then drain and toss with 1 tablespoon of the oil.

Heat the remaining oil in a wok or large frying pan and sauté the onion, cabbage, garlic, and fresh chillies for 2 minutes. Add the prawns, the noodles, pork, light soy sauce, fish sauce, and reserved mushroom liquid. Stir until heated through, then place in a serving dish and garnish with the spring onions.

Gudyo Pat

Thai noodle dishes can be very complex, like *pathai* (see page 122), or quite simple. This one has all the basic tastes of Thai food except the spicy heat. You can use chicken or prawns instead of pork, or for that matter parboiled vegetables.

1 lb (500 g) wide, flat egg noodles
3 tablespoons groundnut oil, or as
needed
8 cloves garlic, peeled and
chopped
4 oz (125 g) lean pork, thinly
shredded

1 teaspoon fish sauce,* or to taste
1 teaspoon granulated sugar
2 tablespoons soy sauce
3 spring onions, chopped

Cook the noodles *al dente* (see page 26), then drain them and dry on paper towels.

Fry the chopped garlic in groundnut oil until brown, then add the pork shreds and cook until brown as well.

Add the noodles and fry until lightly browned, then add the fish sauce, sugar, and soy sauce and heat through. Garnish with the spring onions and serve.

Thai 'Wet' and 'Dry' Noodles

Like other Thai and Southeast Asian noodle dishes, this one is served either 'wet', with soup, or 'dry', as a noodle garnish. This method of double-cooking pork is very common in Chinese cooking as well.

8 oz (250 g) pork tenderloin, fat removed
2 tablespoons groundnut oil
3 cloves garlic, peeled and thinly sliced
2 fresh green chillies, seeded and finely chopped
½ teaspoon crushed dried red chillies*
Fish sauce* to taste
1 teaspoon granulated sugar
Vinegar to taste

2–3 oz (60–90 g) dry-roasted peanuts (roasted without oil – use ordinary roasted nuts if you cannot find them)
4 spring onions, chopped
8 tablespoons chopped fresh coriander
Bean sprouts, washed and picked over (optional)
1½ pints (750 ml) chicken or other stock (for 'wet' – optional)
1 lb (500 g) narrow, flat noodles

Boil the pork until cooked through, about 20 minutes, then drain and slice thin. Set aside.

Heat the oil in a wok and fry the garlic until golden. Add the sliced pork, fresh and dried chillies, fish sauce, sugar, and vinegar. Cook briefly, stirring.

Meanwhile, boil the noodles *al dente* (see page 26). Drain and place in individual bowls. Add the meat mixture to each bowl, then garnish with the peanuts, spring onions, coriander, and bean sprouts.

Or, if 'wet', heat the chicken or other stock and pour over the noodles before adding the garnishes.

Spicy Lamb with Vermicelli

This is a simple, Hunam-style recipe: it should be *hot*. You could serve the lamb pieces over soaked, instead of fried, bean thread noodles.

1 lb (500 g) lean lamb, boned
2 teaspoons salt
2 teaspoons cornflour
½ teaspoon granulated sugar
½ pint (250 ml) groundnut oil
2 tablespoons hoisin sauce*
1 tablespoon very finely chopped fresh ginger*

1 teaspoon very finely chopped garlic
2 tablespoons soy sauce
Hot chilli oil* or Tabasco to taste
6 oz (190 g) bean thread noodles*

Cut the lamb into thin shreds and mix with the salt, cornflour, and sugar. Heat the oil in a wok and deep-fry the lamb until browned, then remove with a slotted spoon and drain on paper towels.

Heat the oil again and separate the noodles into small handfuls. Fry each handful quickly, for about 2 seconds, and drain well.

Remove all but 2 tablespoons of the oil and heat. Stir-fry the ginger and garlic briefly, then add the soy sauce, hoisin sauce, and hot chilli oil or Tabasco. Place the noodles in a bowl, top with the lamb, and pour the sauce over. Toss and serve.

Peking Noodles

Peking noodles was the dish that first introduced me to northern Chinese cooking, and I feel quite sentimental about it. It is also invariably appetizing and quite filling.

1 tablespoon groundnut oil
8 oz (250 g) minced beef

3 cloves garlic, very finely chopped

2 tablespoons dry sherry

1 bunch spring onions, finely chopped (about 8 tablespoons)

3 tablespoons hoisin sauce*

2 tablespoons soy sauce

1 teaspoon vinegar

8 tablespoons water

1 lb (500 g) fresh Chinese noodles* or spaghetti

1 cucumber, peeled, sliced in half, seeded, and shredded, for garnish

8 oz (250 g) bean sprouts, washed and picked over, for garnish

2 spring onions, chopped, for garnish

Heat the oil in a wok, then stir-fry the beef and the garlic until both are browned and the beef is broken up. Pour off all but about 2 tablespoons of the fat. Add the sherry, spring onions, hoisin sauce, soy sauce, and vinegar and let simmer. Add the water and bring back to a simmer.

Meanwhile, boil the noodles *al dente* (see page 26) and drain well. Serve with the sauce on top and the garnishes separately.

Noodles with Ma Po Bean Curd

Ma po is my favourite way of eating bean curd. It is a hot, peppery pork sauce with lumps of bean curd in it, subtly flavoured with perfumy, smoky Szechuan brown peppercorns. Served with noodles, it is a filling meal.

5 squares fresh bean curd*

8 oz (250 g) minced pork

1 tablespoon finely chopped garlic

3 spring onions, finely chopped

1 tablespoon chilli paste with garlic*

2 tablespoons soy sauce

1 teaspoon salt

½ pint (250 ml) water or stock

1 teaspoon Szechuan brown peppercorns,* [1] pulverized in a mortar

1 lb (500 g) fresh Chinese noodles* or spaghetti

2 teaspoons cornflour mixed with 2 teaspoons cold water

1 tablespoon sesame oil*

[1] If you can't buy them use ordinary black peppercorns instead.

Cut the bean curd into ½-inch (1-cm) cubes and set aside.

In a dry, heavy frying pan or wok, fry the minced pork over a high heat, stirring to separate as it browns. Add the garlic, spring onions, chilli paste, soy sauce, salt, stock or water, pepper, and bean curd and bring just to the boil. Simmer for about 10 minutes.

Meanwhile, boil the noodles *al dente* (see page 26), drain well, and place in a serving bowl.

Add the cornflour mixture to the bean curd mixture and stir very gently, over a medium heat, until the mixture thickens. Sprinkle with the sesame oil and serve, tossed with the noodles.

Sha-Cha Beef Noodles

Friends who have lived in Taiwan remember making this, or buying bowls of it late at night from noodle stalls, where it is made to order. This is only one version of the dish, and this one has its own variations: you can make it 'dry' or 'wet' with beef stock. The 'barbecue sauce' that is called for is *nothing* like our barbecue sauces, so don't use them. Chinese bottled 'barbecue sauce' is made from sesame oil and dried shrimp, among other things.

8 oz (250 g) lean beef, shredded
2 tablespoons cornflour
½ teaspoon salt
Pinch of granulated sugar
2 tablespoons soy sauce
1 lb (500 g) fresh Chinese noodles* or spaghetti
2 tablespoons groundnut oil, more if necessary
8 oz (250 g) mustard greens,

Chinese cabbage,* or ordinary cabbage, washed and shredded
4 spring onions, chopped
2 tablespoons 'barbecue sauce'*
1½ pints (750 ml) hot beef stock (for 'wet' – optional), mixed with 1 tablespoon soy sauce
2 tablespoons chopped spring onions for garnish

Combine the beef with the cornflour, salt, sugar, and soy sauce in a small bowl. Set aside.

Cook the noodles *al dente* (see page 26), then drain well.

Heat the oil in a wok or heavy frying pan and fry the beef mixture in it for about 2 minutes, stirring. Remove the beef with a slotted spoon and set aside.

Add more oil if necessary, then add the greens and stir-fry over a high heat. Add the spring onions and stir-fry briefly, then add the 'barbecue sauce' and stir for 1 minute.

Place noodles in individual bowls and top with the meat and vegetables. (If the 'wet' version is desired, pour the beef stock and soy sauce mixture over the noodles.) Garnish with the chopped spring onion and serve.

Thopa (Tibetan Noodle Dish)

In Tibet, noodles are a staple food. I learned this recipe from Pasang Sherpa in Kathmandu, a man who makes a fine muscatel wine, and who is, I think, a true Renaissance man. Noodles are often used in ceremonial occasions, like the mid-winter 'noodle day' on which the Gu-thu is eaten. On the twenty-ninth day of the twelfth month a special form of noodles is made, the Gu-thu, into which are put stones, a piece of wood, wool, and other things, all wrapped in dough. When the bowls of noodles are served, one opens one's dough lump and the item one receives is an indication of one's fortune. One of them means that the recipient has to provide barley beer for all the rest. Traditionally, one eats nine bowls of this, and there are chants to go with the bowls, such as 'Having eaten the Gu-thu who cares if one is ill! Having eaten the Gu-thu who cares if one dies!'

The chillies in this dish make it fairly hot, so use fewer if you prefer.

8 oz (250 g) lean beef, very thinly shredded

2 cloves garlic, very finely chopped

2 tablespoons groundnut oil

5 fresh red or green chillies, finely chopped

6 to 8 spring onions, cut into thin shreds, 2 inches (5 cm) long

2 tablespoons shredded fresh ginger*

2 medium carrots, scraped and cut into shreds 2 inches (5 cm) long

2 pints (1 litre) beef or chicken stock

1 green pepper, seeded and shredded

Salt to taste

1 lb (500 g) thin egg noodles

Combine the beef shreds with the garlic. Heat the oil in a heavy frying pan and stir-fry the beef shreds quickly until brown, then add half the chillies, half the spring onions, and half the ginger and stir-fry for 2 minutes. Add the carrots and stir-fry for 2 minutes more.

Bring the stock to a simmer in another pan and add the remaining chillies and ginger, the shredded green pepper, and salt to taste.

Meanwhile, boil the egg noodles *al dente* (see page 26). Drain, then divide between soup bowls. Add some of the meat mixture to each, pour the soup over, and garnish with the remaining spring onions. Serve immediately.

Soba with Chinese Sausages, Peas, and Mushrooms

This is an invention combining a love of Japanese soba noodles and Chinese pork sausages. The slightly sweet soup mixture is also 'Japanese'. A very aesthetic dish – dark reddish sausages, light green peas, and black mushrooms against pale green noodles.

1 lb (500 g) soba noodles*	2 tablespoons soy sauce
1 bag dashi*	1 tablespoon very finely chopped
¾ pint (375 ml) water	fresh ginger*
10 dried mushrooms,* soaked in	1 teaspoon salt
hot water for 30 minutes,	1 teaspoon granulated sugar
soaking liquid reserved	4 oz (125 g) frozen peas
3 Chinese sausages,* sliced and	3 spring onions, chopped
steamed for 5 minutes	

Boil the noodles *al dente* (see page 26) and drain well.

Put the dashi bag in the boiling water and simmer for 20 minutes, then add the mushrooms, reserved mushroom liquid, and sausages and simmer for 2 minutes. Add the soy sauce, ginger, salt, and sugar, then add the peas and cook for 4 minutes. Place the noodles in a serving bowl and pour the sausage mixture over. Garnish with the spring onions and serve.

Egg Vermicelli and Sausages

One of the basic noodle-cooking methods in Asia involves precooking the noodles and then frying them over a high heat with quick-cooking ingredients, until they are browned and crisp in places. Like fried rice, this dish has a last minute, 'scrambled' egg addition.

12 oz (375 g) thin egg vermicelli (see note below)	3 Chinese sausages,* thinly sliced
3 eggs	1 tablespoon very finely chopped fresh ginger*
1 tablespoon soy sauce	½ teaspoon granulated sugar
1 teaspoon sesame oil*	Salt to taste
3 tablespoons groundnut oil	3 spring onions, chopped

Boil the noodles *al dente*. (These take only a few minutes – sometimes only 4.) Drain well.

Beat the eggs with the soy sauce and sesame oil. Set aside.

Heat the groundnut oil in a wok or heavy frying pan. Sauté the sausages and ginger for 2 minutes, stirring, then add the drained noodles and stir-fry until they brown in places. Add the sugar, salt, and spring onions and then, stirring, the egg mixture. Stir-fry until eggs are cooked. Serve at once.

Note: Filipino grocers have some called 'angel's hair', in skeins.

Spinach and Pork with Noodles

Spinach and pork are an excellent noodle combination. This recipe is quite simple, and exploits the flavours well.

1 tablespoon dry sherry
2 tablespoons soy sauce
1 teaspoon granulated sugar
1 teaspoon salt
8 oz (250 g) pork tenderloin, shredded
8 dried mushrooms*

2 tablespoons groundnut oil
8 oz (250 g) fresh spinach, washed and picked over
2 spring onions, chopped
1 lb (500 g) fresh Chinese noodles* or spaghetti
2 teaspoons sesame oil*

Combine the sherry, soy sauce, sugar, and salt in a bowl and add the pork shreds. Let marinate for 1 hour.

Soak the dried mushrooms in warm water for 20 minutes, then squeeze dry and slice.

Heat the groundnut oil in a wok or heavy frying pan and stir-fry the pork and mushrooms for 5 minutes. Add the spinach and spring onions, then cover and let cook over a high heat, just until the spinach is wilted.

Meanwhile, boil the noodles *al dente* (see page 25), drain well and toss with sesame oil. Serve immediately, tossed with the pork and spinach mixture.

Kuksoo Bibim I

Korean noodle dishes are very delicious, and there are many variations on the basic garlic, sesame, and chilli combination of seasonings. Here are two versions, one with minced pork and the other with shredded beef, of the classic bean thread noodle dish.

8 oz (250 g) bean thread noodles*
8 oz (250 g) minced pork
3 tablespoons soy sauce
2 teaspoons granulated sugar
2 tablespoons chopped spring onions
3 cloves garlic, very finely chopped
4 teaspoons sesame seeds
1 tablespoon sesame oil*

3 cucumbers, peeled, cut in half lengthwise, and seeded
½ teaspoon salt
1½ tablespoons groundnut oil
1 spring onion, very finely chopped
Cayenne pepper to taste
2 eggs, beaten
½ pint (250 ml) beef bouillon

Boil the noodles for 3 or 4 minutes, then drain them well. Cool with cold water and drain again.

Heat a wok or heavy frying pan and stir-fry the pork, separating it as it browns. Add 2 tablespoons of the soy sauce, the sugar, the 2 tablespoons chopped spring onions and the minced garlic. Stir in 2 teaspoons of the sesame seeds, crushed in a mortar, and the sesame oil and set aside.

Cut the cucumbers into long thin pieces, then into 2-inch (5-cm) lengths, and add salt. Heat 1 tablespoon of the groundnut oil in another frying pan. Add the cucumbers and stir-fry briefly with the finely chopped spring onion, the remaining sesame seeds, the cayenne, and the remaining tablespoon of soy sauce. Remove from the heat.

In a flat frying pan, heat the $\frac{1}{2}$ tablespoon groundnut oil and fry the eggs into a pancake. Let cool, then cut into thin strips.

Reheat the pork mixture, add the bouillon, and bring to a simmer.

Place the noodles in individual bowls. Add some cucumber mixture to each, then some meat mixture, and garnish with egg and more spring onion.

Kuksoo Bibim II

This is the shredded beef version.

8 oz (250 g) beef, shredded
3 tablespoons soy sauce
2 tablespoons sesame oil*
1½ tablespoons sesame seeds, crushed in a mortar
2 tablespoons granulated sugar
Salt and freshly ground black pepper

2 cloves garlic, very finely chopped
2 teaspoons groundnut oil
1 cucumber, peeled, cut in half lengthwise, seeded, and cut into strips
2 medium eggs
8 oz (250 g) bean thread noodles*

Mix the beef shreds with the soy sauce, sesame oil, sesame seeds, sugar, salt, pepper, and garlic. Heat in a wok or heavy frying pan seasoned with the groundnut oil.

Beat the eggs lightly and fry into a pancake in a flat frying pan, then cool and cut into narrow strips.

Combine the beef, cucumber, and egg and set aside while you boil the noodles *al dente* (see page 26). Drain and place in a bowl, then cover with the beef mixture and serve.

Chungking Pork with Noodles

Chungking pork, though not usually served with noodles, has a definite affinity for them. A common addition to this dish is salted, fermented black beans, rinsed, dried and *slightly* mashed.

8 oz (250 g) lean pork
¾ pint (375 ml) water
1 teaspoon dry sherry
1 tablespoon very finely chopped fresh ginger*
3 tablespoons groundnut oil
12 oz (375 g) sliced green cabbage
4 tablespoons crushed yellow beans*

3 tablespoons soy sauce
2 teaspoons dried red chillies*
2 cloves garlic, very finely chopped
1 lb (500 g) fresh Chinese noodles* or spaghetti

Simmer the pork in a small saucepan with the water, the sherry, and 1 tablespoon of the ginger until tender. Let the pork cool in the saucepan, then cut into large slices. Reserve the cooking liquid.

Place half the oil in a wok or saucepan over a medium heat. Add the cabbage and stir-fry for about 1 minute, or until partially translucent. Remove and set aside.

Add the remaining oil to the wok or saucepan, then add the crushed yellow beans, soy sauce, dried red chillies, garlic, pork, and pork stock. Cook, stirring, for another minute.

Meanwhile, cook the noodles *al dente* (see page 26) and drain well.

Return the cabbage to the pork mixture, pour the sauce over the noodles, and serve immediately.

Stir-fried Noodles with
Chinese Sausage and Dried Shrimp

Chinese pork and liver sausages, the small, hard ones, have become a staple in my house. They have a subtle aniseed flavour – a kind of Chinese peperoni – and are not too spicy. They keep in the refrigerator for weeks, freeze well, and are delicious wherever you include them. Dried shrimp, with their interesting fishiness, are a great foil for them.

1 lb (500 g) fresh Chinese
  noodles* or spaghetti
2 tablespoons sesame oil*
4 oz (125 g) dried shrimp*
4 Chinese sausages

2 tablespoons groundnut oil
1 bunch spring onions, chopped
  (about 8 tablespoons)
3 tablespoons soy sauce

Boil fresh noodles for 5 minutes, then drain, toss with the sesame oil, and set aside. (If you are using dried ones boil just *al dente* and drain well.)

Soak the dried shrimp in water for about an hour.

Slice the sausages and steam in a colander or vegetable steamer basket for 5 minutes over boiling water. (This removes excess fat.)

Heat the groundnut oil in a wok or heavy frying pan. Add the noodles and stir-fry over a high heat until they begin to brown. Add the drained shrimp, spring onions, sausages, and soy sauce and stir over a medium heat until heated through. Serve immediately.

Kung Lo Mein, Burmese Style

1 teaspoon sesame oil*
4 tablespoons groundnut oil
8 cloves garlic, peeled and sliced
8 oz (250 g) duck, pork, or chicken
  meat, cooked and cut into small
  cubes
8 oz (250 g) Chinese cabbage,*
  shredded

8 oz (250 g) spinach, shredded
3 spring onions, chopped
3 fresh green chillies, seeded and
  finely chopped
1 lb (500 g) fresh Chinese
  noodles* or spaghetti

Heat the oils in a wok until very hot. Drop in the garlic pieces and fry them until brown; *do not let them burn*. Remove with a slotted spoon and drain on paper towels.

Remove all but 2 tablespoons of oil from the wok. Heat, add the meat, and stir-fry until browned. Reduce the heat and add the cabbage, spinach, spring onions, and chillies and stir-fry for 2 minutes, or until the spinach wilts.

Boil the noodles *al dente* (see page 25), then drain and toss with the meat and vegetable mixture. Sprinkle with the crisp garlic bits and serve.

Pork and Bean Sprout Lo Mein

A well-made *lo mein* dish, using fresh ingredients and assembled at the last minute, is a treat. The twice-cooked noodles with their crisp, brown edges are splendid tossed with crisp sautéed vegetables. Nothing like the versions served in 'greasy chopstick' places.

8 oz (250 g) pork tenderloin, shredded
1 tablespoon cornflour
1 tablespoon soy sauce
1 lb (500 g) thin fresh Chinese noodles* or spaghetti
Sesame oil*
2 tablespoons groundnut oil
½ tin (1 lb 3 oz (590 g)) bamboo shoots,* cut into thin strips

8 oz (250 g) bean sprouts, washed and picked over
1 teaspoon salt
1 bunch spring onions, chopped (about 8 tablespoons)
2 tablespoons finely chopped fresh coriander or flat parsley

Combine the pork with the cornflour and soy sauce. Set aside.

Boil the noodles *al dente* (see page 26), then drain well in a colander and run cold water over them. Place in a bowl and toss with 1 tablespoon sesame oil. Set aside.

Heat the groundnut oil in a large wok or frying pan. Add the pork and stir-fry over a high heat for 2 minutes, until the shreds separate and are browned. Add the bamboo shoots, lower the heat to medium, and stir-fry for 1 minute. Add the noodles and raise the heat, tossing the mixture often until some of the noodles are browned and they are all heated through.

Add the bean sprouts and stir-fry for 2 minutes. Add the salt and toss, then add the spring onions, fresh coriander or parsley, and sesame oil to taste and toss well. Serve immediately.

Meat Kreplach

Even if one has one's grandmother's recipe for these, they never have quite the same taste. These come close to my grandmother's and perhaps to yours. Like wonton, like tortellini and ravioli, these are a staple of sorts, and can be served in a number of different ways: baked as an appetizer or with a light tomato sauce, or, best of all, I think, floating in a perfect chicken soup.

Noodle Dough
2 eggs
½ teaspoon salt

8 oz (250 g) plain flour
1 tablespoon water

Meat Filling
2 tablespoons rendered chicken fat (see note below)
1 small onion, finely chopped
1 lb (500 g) minced lean beef

Salt and freshly ground pepper to taste
1 egg

To make the noodle dough, beat the eggs in a bowl and add the salt, flour, and water. Knead until smooth and elastic, adding more flour

if necessary. Form into a ball and set aside, covered with a clean cloth, for 30 minutes.

For the filling, heat the chicken fat in a frying pan and sauté the onion until golden. Add the meat and cook, stirring to separate it, until it is brown. Add salt and pepper and remove from the heat. Let cool, then beat in the egg.

To form the kreplach, roll the dough out on a floured board or tabletop until very thin. Cut into 2-inch (5-cm) squares and place a teaspoonful of meat mixture on each square. Fold the dough over the meat to form a triangle and pinch the edges together hard, moistening with water if necessary to make a good seal. Press the two corners at the base of the triangle together and set aside on a towel.

Cook the kreplach in boiling salted water for about 20 minutes before adding to soup, sautéing in groundnut oil, or baking.

Note: Rendering fat means extracting fat from meat trimmings. Cut them up small and either place in a cool oven until the fat has melted out or boil them in an uncovered pan with very little water until the water has boiled away and the fat has melted. Strain the fat into a basin.

Hungarian Layered Noodles

Every time we make this dish it turns out differently, depending on the sausages available, what cheeses we use, and so forth. The long baking merges the flavours nicely. Always delicious, and a fine winter supper.

3 medium potatoes, peeled and cut into chunks

8 oz (250 g) butter, melted

8 oz (250 g) large macaroni, shells or ziti, boiled *al dente*

6 hard-boiled eggs, quartered

8 oz (250 g) bacon, sautéed until crisp and drained

8 oz (250 g) cured ham, sliced

1 lb (500 g) hot Italian sausages,* cut into chunks

1 pint (500 ml) sour cream

Gruyère cheese, freshly grated

Salt and freshly ground black pepper to taste

1 oz (30 g) breadcrumbs

Boil the potatoes in salted water just until tender, then drain and toss with 2 tablespoons of the butter.

Boil the pasta *al dente* (see page 26), then drain and toss with another 2 tablespoons of the butter.

Preheat the oven to 325°F (160°C), mark 3.

In a buttered casserole, layer the potatoes, eggs, pasta, bacon, ham, sausages, sour cream, and cheese. Add salt and pepper to taste, using plenty of pepper. Top with the breadcrumbs and pour the remaining butter over, then bake for 2 hours, or until bubbly. Keep the heat low; it should take at least 1½ hours to get browned·

Portuguese Marinated Pork and Mussel Sauce with Spaghetti

Marinating pork in wine and herbs makes it a different sort of animal. This preparation is often used in 'mock' game recipes. Here, with mussels it makes a very interesting sauce for spaghetti.

1 lb (500 g) boneless pork, cut into thin strips 2 inches (5 cm) long
8 tablespoons dry white wine
2 cloves garlic, peeled and crushed
Salt and freshly ground pepper to taste
1 teaspoon chopped fresh thyme or ½ teaspoon dried
½ teaspoon cayenne pepper
2 tablespoons groundnut oil
1 lb (500 g) mussels, scrubbed and debearded
1 lb (500 g) spaghetti
Butter

Marinate the pork strips in the wine, garlic, salt and pepper, thyme, and cayenne. Set aside for 2 or 3 hours in the refrigerator.

Drain the pork, reserving the marinade, then pat dry with paper towels. Heat the oil in a heavy saucepan and sauté the pork until well browned. Add the reserved marinade and cover. Simmer for 20 minutes, then add the mussels and cover. Cook until the mussels open, about 10 minutes.

Meanwhile, boil the spaghetti *al dente* (see page 26) and drain well. Toss with butter, then top with the pork and mussels, arranging the mussels on top and pouring the sauce over them.

Tanzanian Pork and Plantain Noodles

Plantains are used in much Caribbean and African cooking, and are worth experimenting with. They are available in many city markets. Try them baked, sautéed, or in this African curry.

6 plantains (or use green bananas)
3 tablespoons groundnut oil
1 large onion, finely chopped
1 lb (500 g) pork tenderloin, cut into 1-inch (2½-cm) chunks
2 large tomatoes, peeled, seeded, and chopped (see note on page 49)
2 large green peppers, seeded and chopped

1 tablespoon imported curry powder, preferably Madras
¾ pint (375 ml) water
Salt and freshly ground pepper to taste
1 lb (500 g) string beans, ends removed and broken into 2-inch (5-cm) pieces
1 lb (500 g) broad egg noodles

Skin and slice the plantains or bananas and place in a bowl with water to cover (to keep them from browning).

Heat oil in a large, heavy saucepan. Add the pork and onions and brown, stirring. Add the tomatoes, green peppers, curry powder and water. Simmer for 30 minutes, then add salt and pepper, the plantains or bananas, and the string beans. Simmer for 15 minutes or more, until the vegetables are done.

Boil the noodles *al dente* (see page 26), then drain. Pour the sauce over to serve.

Bassi (Ethiopian Beef and Squash Sauce for Noodles)

Yellow summer squash and beef in a spicy, peanutty sauce may seem a little strange to our tastes, but it is a delicious concoction. Ethiopian stews, like Nigerian and some other African dishes, use peanuts both as a thickener and as a source of protein. With beans, beef, peanuts, and noodles, this dish is as protein-rich as you could want.

2 tablespoons groundnut oil
2 medium onions, chopped
2 cloves garlic, very finely chopped
1 lb (500 g) boneless beef, cut into 1-inch (2- or 3-cm) chunks
2 tablespoons tomato paste
1½ tins (14 oz (440 g) size) haricot or white pea beans or 8 oz (250 g) dried beans, soaked overnight and cooked until tender

1 large green pepper or sweet red pepper, seeded and diced
8 oz (250 g) peanut butter
Tabasco to taste
8 oz (250 g) summer squash, cut into 2-inch (5-cm) cubes
Salt and freshly ground pepper to taste
1 lb (500 g) broad egg noodles

Heat the oil in a heavy saucepan and sauté the onion and garlic. Add the beef and sauté for about 3 minutes, until the colour changes. Add the tomato paste, beans, and green pepper, then add water to cover the ingredients and simmer, uncovered, for 40 minutes. Let the sauce reduce to about ¾ pint (375 ml).

Mix the peanut butter and Tabasco with a little water to thin. Add, along with the squash and salt and pepper, to the mixture in the saucepan. Simmer for 15 minutes more, or until the beef is tender.

Meanwhile, boil the noodles *al dente* (see page 26). Drain well, then pour the sauce over and serve.

Tunisian Lamb Balls with Noodles

Tunisian lamb recipes, like Persian meat dishes, often include a fruit. Apricot jam may seem a doubtful ingredient, but it is perfectly suited to this dish.

2 medium onions
1 lb (500 g) minced lamb
1 tablespoon finely chopped fresh mint or 1 teaspoon dried
½ teaspoon ground cumin
1 tablespoon very finely chopped fresh parsley
Salt and freshly ground black pepper to taste

1 egg
Plain flour for coating
3 tablespoons groundnut oil
1 oz (30 g) butter
½ lb (250 g) apricot jam, heated and sieved
3 tablespoons lemon juice
1 lb (500 g) very thin egg noodles

Put the onions and lamb through a meat mincer, then combine with the mint, cumin, parsley, salt, pepper, and egg. Knead well, then form into small balls and roll in flour to coat.

Heat the oil and butter to bubbling in a heavy frying pan and brown the meatballs well.

Combine the apricot jam and lemon juice in a small saucepan and heat to a simmer.

Cook the noodles *al dente* (see page 26), then drain and place in a serving dish. Arrange the meatballs on the noodles, then top with the apricot sauce and serve.

Pork and String Bean Goulash with Noodles

Pork, sour cream and crisp sautéed string beans make a delicious sauce for noodles. Marinating the pork in vinegar (you could use dry white wine) is a trick I learned from the Portuguese dish of marinated pork and mussels on page 162.

1 lb (500 g) pork tenderloin, cut into ½-inch (1-cm) cubes
2 tablespoons white wine vinegar
3 cloves garlic, very finely chopped
½ teaspoon dried thyme
Salt and freshly ground black pepper to taste
1 oz (30 g) butter
12 oz (375 g) fresh string beans, ends removed and broken into 1-inch (2- or 3-cm) pieces

2 tablespoons olive oil
3 medium onions, thinly sliced
1 tablespoon imported Hungarian paprika
4 tablespoons dry white wine
12 oz (375 g) macaroni (gemelli, for example)
½ pint (250 ml) sour cream
4 tablespoons chopped chives

Place the pork in a glass or glazed bowl and add the vinegar, garlic, thyme, salt, and pepper. Set aside for 1 hour.

Heat the butter in a large frying pan and sauté the string beans over a high heat, until spottily browned – less than 5 minutes.

In another frying pan, heat the oil and sauté the onions slowly, until browned and soft. Add the paprika and salt and pepper to the onions, then add the pork and the marinade. Raise the heat, stirring, to boil off the liquid and brown.

Add the white wine and simmer until the pork is tender, then reduce the heat and toss in the string beans.

Meanwhile, boil the macaroni *al dente* (see page 26) and drain.

Add the sour cream to the pork and beans and stir well. Season to taste, then serve over the noodles, garnished with chives.

Espagueti con Salchichas

This is a Caribbean/Spanish version of spaghetti with sausages, made more lively with chillies, olives, and capers. The sauce is best when made the day before serving, and a teaspoon or so of fresh lemon juice helps too.

2 tablespoons groundnut oil or margarine

1 tablespoon finely chopped salt pork

1 or 2 oz (30–60 g) ham, roughly
  chopped
1 medium onion, finely chopped
1 medium tomato, roughly
  chopped
1 green pepper, seeded and
  chopped
3 small fresh green chillies, seeded
  and chopped

8 green olives, pitted and chopped
1 teaspoon capers
8 oz (250 g) garlic sausage or hot
  Italian pork sausage*
1 8 oz (250 g) tin Italian plum
  tomatoes, blended until smooth
1 lb (500 g) spaghetti

Heat the oil or margarine in a heavy saucepan and brown the salt
pork and ham for about 3 minutes. Add the onion, tomato, green
pepper, fresh chillies, olives, and capers and cook slowly for 5
minutes. Cut the sausage into small chunks and add, along with
the tomato purée. Cook for 5 minutes longer, stirring.

Meanwhile, boil the spaghetti *al dente* (see page 26). Drain well
and serve with the sauce and freshly grated Parmesan cheese.

Chilli with Macaroni

Chilli with macaroni is an old standby, but no less delicious and
welcome for that. You can assemble this, and refrigerate or freeze
before baking.

2 tablespoons olive oil
3 medium onions, chopped
1 lb (500 g) minced beef
2 stalks celery, chopped
2 green peppers, seeded and
  chopped
Oregano, chilli powder, and
  thyme or savory to taste
1 teaspoon granulated sugar

1 large tin (28 oz (875 g) size)
  Italian plum tomatoes, plus 1
  small tin (8 oz (250 g) size)
  roughly chopped
3 tins (14 oz (440 g) size) red
  kidney beans, drained
1 lb (500 g) small macaroni
3 tablespoons chopped fresh coriander

Heat the oil in a heavy saucepan. Sauté the onions until browned,
then add the beef, breaking up the lumps as it browns. Add the
celery, green peppers, oregano, chilli powder, thyme or savory, sugar,

and tomatoes. Cook for about 20 minutes, then add the kidney beans and cook for 10 minutes longer.

Preheat the oven to 350°F (175°C), mark 4.

Boil the macaroni *al dente* (see page 26) and drain well. Toss with the chilli mixture, place in a buttered casserole, and bake for 40 minutes.

Macarrones con Costillitas de Cerdo

Like the Caribbean spaghetti with sausages, this dish contains olives and capers, which distinguishes it from a plain tomato sauce. A messy dish to eat, for you have the bones of the spareribs to negotiate. Large cloth napkins are a necessity.

1 oz (30 g) margarine creamed with 1 teaspoon Hungarian paprika
3 oz (90 g) smoked ham, chopped
1 tablespoon finely chopped salt pork
1 green pepper, seeded and chopped
1 onion, finely chopped
1 8 oz (250 g) tin Italian plum tomatoes, blended until smooth
2 lb (1 kg) spareribs, cut into ribs and chopped in half

1 tablespoon plus 1 teaspoon salt
15 pitted black olives
1 tablespoon drained capers
½ pint (250 ml) water
1 lb (500 g) elbow macaroni
1 tablespoon olive oil
1 14 oz (440 g) tin plus 1 8 oz (250 g) tin Italian plum tomatoes
2 oz (60 g) Parmesan cheese, freshly grated

Heat the margarine in a large, heavy saucepan. Add the ham, salt pork, green pepper, and onion and sauté quickly until the onion is browned. Add the tomato purée, spareribs, 1 teaspoon of the salt, olives, capers, and water, then cover and simmer for 40 minutes, adding more water if necessary.

Meanwhile, cook the macaroni *al dente* (see page 26) in boiling water to which has been added the olive oil and the remaining tablespoon of salt. Drain well.

Add the whole tomatoes and macaroni to the sauce and cook, covered, for 15 minutes. Then toss with the cheese and serve.

Calf's Liver Smetana

However enlightened and, perhaps, impoverished we become, we still don't use innards enough. This is a Hungarian recipe in which you can substitute chicken livers just as well.

12 oz (375 g) calf's liver, partly frozen, sliced very thin

1 oz (30 g) plain flour, seasoned with salt and freshly ground black pepper to taste

1 medium onion, finely chopped

5 bacon rashers

1 teaspoon dried thyme

1 lb (500 g) medium egg noodles

½ pint (250 ml) sour cream

Chopped fresh parsley for garnish

Sauté the bacon until crisp in a heavy frying pan. Drain on paper towels, then pour off all but 2 tablespoons of the fat from the frying pan.

Sauté the onion in the bacon fat until golden, then add the calf's liver, first dredged in the seasoned flour, and toss for 5 minutes, until cooked through. Crumble the bacon in, then add the thyme and more salt and pepper to taste. Remove from the heat.

Boil noodles *al dente* (see page 26), then drain and place in a serving bowl.

Reheat the liver mixture briefly. Add the sour cream and blend well, taking care not to let the mixture boil. Pour over the noodles and toss, then serve, garnished with parsley.

Pastitsio

Pastitsio is a Greek version of baked macaroni and beef casserole. The white sauce topping is different, however, and reminiscent of the topping for moussaka, and the addition of cinnamon and nutmeg to the meat mixture gives a hint of Middle Eastern influence.

1 oz (30 g) butter
2 tablespoons olive oil
1 large onion, chopped
8 oz (250 g) minced beef
8 oz (250 g) minced lamb
8 tablespoons dry white wine
½ small tin (8 oz (250 g) size)
  Italian plum tomatoes, blended
  until smooth
3 tablespoons tomato paste
2 cloves garlic, finely chopped
½ teaspoon ground cinnamon
1 teaspoon dried oregano
¼ teaspoon freshly grated nutmeg

Salt and freshly ground black
  pepper to taste
3 medium tomatoes, peeled,
  seeded, and roughly chopped
  (see note on page 49)
1 oz (30 g) fresh breadcrumbs
1 lb (500 g) macaroni
3 oz (90 g) Parmesan cheese,
  freshly grated
¾ pint (375 ml) White Sauce (page
  227)
¾ pint (375 ml) Tomato Paste
  Sauce (page 226)

Heat the butter and oil together in a large frying pan and cook the onion until golden. Add the minced beef and lamb and cook, stirring to break up lumps, until browned. Pour off any extra fat, then add the wine, tomato purée, tomato paste, garlic, cinnamon, oregano, nutmeg, salt, pepper, and tomatoes and simmer for 10 minutes, or until thick, over a low heat. Stir in the breadcrumbs and set aside.

Preheat the oven to 400°F (200°C), mark 6.

Boil macaroni *al dente* (see page 26) and drain. Put half the macaroni into a buttered casserole and sprinkle on 4 tablespoons of the Parmesan. Add all the meat sauce and cover with the remaining macaroni. Sprinkle on another 4 tablespoons Parmesan, then cover with the white sauce and sprinkle with the remaining Parmesan. Bake for 35 minutes or until browned, then cut into squares and serve with the homemade tomato sauce.

Veal Paprikash

Hungarian goulashes and other meat stews with sour cream are best served with the slightly curly, flat egg noodles. An alternative method of preparation involves marinating the veal for an hour in he wine, herbs, onions, and garlic before browning it.

2 oz (60 g) butter
2 onions, very finely chopped
4 cloves garlic, very finely
   chopped
2 lb (1 kg) veal stew meat, cut into
   1-inch (2- or 3-cm) chunks
1 bay leaf
1 teaspoon dried thyme
½ pint (250 ml) dry white wine
Salt and freshly ground black
   pepper to taste

3 tablespoons sweet Hungarian
   paprika
2 teaspoons tomato paste
1 pint (500 ml) sour cream, at
   room temperature
8 tablespoons chopped fresh dill
   or 1 tablespoon dried dillweed
1 lb (500 g) curly egg noodles

Heat half the butter in a heavy saucepan. Add the onion and garlic and stir over a medium heat until browned, then add the veal and stir while browning. Add the bay leaf, thyme, wine, salt, pepper, and paprika and bring to a simmer. Stir in the tomato paste, add water if necessary to cover the meat, and cover the pan. Cook over a low heat until the meat is tender, about 30 or 40 minutes.

Boil the egg noodles *al dente* (see page 26), then drain and toss with the remaining butter. Stir the sour cream and dill into the stew and serve over the noodles.

POULTRY

Chicken Liver Sauce for Egg Noodles

The simplest possible sauce – and quite luxurious tasting. Use good sherry or Marsala. It will be obvious if you haven't. This is also good (and traditional) with gnocchi.

1 lb (500 g) chicken livers
Plain flour, seasoned with salt and freshly ground black pepper to taste
1½ oz (45 g) butter
8 tablespoons dry sherry or Marsala

¼ pint (125 ml) double cream
1 lb (500 g) egg noodles
2 tablespoons chopped fresh parsley

Cut the chicken livers into chunks and dredge with the seasoned flour. Heat the butter to bubbling in a frying pan and sauté the chicken livers briefly. Add the sherry or Marsala, then reduce the liquid over a medium heat for 3 minutes.

Boil the noodles *al dente* (see page 26) and drain.

Add the cream to the sauce and bring to the boil rapidly. Boil for 2 minutes, then add salt and pepper to taste and pour over the noodles. Garnish with the parsley and serve.

Turkey Noodle Casserole

A simple and hearty dish, excellent for leftover turkey. A sort of country cousin to *tetrazzini*.

1 oz (30 g) butter
1 tablespoon vegetable oil

1 medium onion, finely chopped
1 clove garlic, very finely chopped

1 lb (500 g) egg noodles, boiled *al dente* (see page 26) and drained well

1 lb (500 g) cooked dark turkey meat, cut into 1-inch (2- or 3-cm) chunks

Salt and freshly ground black pepper to taste

Brown Sauce (see below)

1 oz (30 g) breadcrumbs mixed with 1 oz (30 g) Parmesan cheese, freshly grated

Preheat the oven to 325°F (160°C), mark 3.

Heat the butter and oil in a heavy frying pan and sauté the onion and garlic until golden. Toss this mixture with the cooked noodles and place in the bottom of a buttered casserole. Add the turkey chunks and salt and pepper to taste, then add brown sauce and top with the breadcrumbs and Parmesan.

Bake until bubbly and browned, 30 to 45 minutes.

Brown Sauce

1 small onion, very finely chopped

½ oz (15 g) butter

1 oz (30 g) plain flour

1 pint (500 ml) beef or turkey stock

½ teaspoon dried thyme

8 tablespoons dry white wine

Salt and freshly ground black pepper to taste

Sauté the onion in the butter until deep brown. Add the flour and cook, stirring, for 2 minutes, then add the beef or turkey stock, thyme, and white wine. Stir as it comes to the boil and begins to thicken, then let it simmer for 20 minutes. Season to taste with salt and pepper; you will have about ¾ pint (375 ml) of sauce.

Turkey Tetrazzini

This is an elegant version of an old standby that is excellent for buffets. It can be frozen or refrigerated before baking.

8 oz (250 g) spaghetti

4 oz (125 g) butter or margarine

3 tablespoons very finely chopped fresh shallots

Salt and freshly ground black pepper to taste

8 oz (250 g) fresh mushrooms, sliced

12 oz (375 g) cooked turkey meat, cut into cubes
1 oz (30 g) plain flour
¾ pint (375 ml) turkey or chicken broth
8 tablespoons double cream
4 tablespoons dry sherry
2 egg yolks
1 oz (30 g) freshly grated Parmesan cheese mixed with ½ oz (15 g) breadcrumbs

Boil the spaghetti *al dente* (see page 26) and drain well. Toss with 1 oz (30 g) of the butter or margarine and set aside.

Heat 1½ oz (45 g) of the butter or margarine in a frying pan and sauté the shallots for 3 minutes, stirring. Add salt and pepper and mushrooms and sauté briefly, until the mushrooms wilt. Place the mixture in a bowl and add the turkey.

Melt the remaining butter or margarine in a saucepan and stir in the flour. Cook, stirring, for a few minutes; do not allow to colour. Add the stock gradually, whisking to keep the mixture smooth, and cook until thick. Simmer gently for 5 minutes, then add salt and pepper to taste. Combine the cream, sherry, and egg yolks in a bowl and gradually whisk in some of the hot sauce. Return the contents of the bowl to the saucepan and heat gently, stirring, over a very low heat for a minute. Taste for seasoning, then combine the sauce with the turkey mixture.

Preheat the oven to 350°F (175°C), mark 4.

Place the spaghetti in a buttered 4-pint (2-litre) casserole. Make a hole in the centre and pour in the turkey mixture, then sprinkle the cheese and breadcrumb mixture over and bake for about 45 minutes, or until browned and bubbly.

Chicken and Peanuts with Noodles

Chicken with all sorts of nuts – almonds, cashews, and especially peanuts – is a feature of Chinese cooking. Be careful when roasting the nuts, because they burn or get dark and bitter very easily.

1 lb (500 g) chicken, boned, skinned and cut into 1-inch (2- or 3-cm) chunks
3 tablespoons groundnut oil
4 oz (125 g) shelled raw peanuts
1 bunch spring onions, chopped (about 8 tablespoons)
4 tablespoons hoisin sauce*

1 tablespoon rice wine vinegar*	2½ teaspoons sesame oil*
2 teaspoons dry sherry	12 oz (375 g) vermicelli or thin
1 teaspoon granulated sugar	egg noodles
3 cloves garlic, very finely chopped	

Sauté the chicken in half the groundnut oil until cooked through.

Place the peanuts on a baking sheet and brown in a 400°F (200°C), mark 6, oven for about 5 minutes, then combine with the spring onions, cooked chicken, hoisin sauce, rice vinegar, sherry, sugar, garlic, and ½ teaspoon of the sesame oil.

Cook the noodles until soft, then drain and add the remaining sesame oil.

Heat the remaining groundnut oil in a wok over a very high flame. Add the noodles and stir-fry for a few minutes, then add the chicken mixture, stir over a high heat for another minute, and serve.

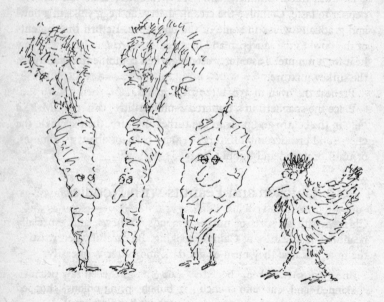

Wholewheat Noodles with Chicken

This eclectic, but delicious, recipe combines Chinese flavourings and Japanese fish/seaweed stock with wholewheat noodles, which you can find in most health food shops.

1½ lb (750 g) chicken (dark meat, not breast)
1 tablespoon cornflour
2 tablespoons groundnut oil
4 tablespoons soy sauce
1 tablespoon sesame oil*
1 tablespoon dry sherry
1 bunch spring onions, chopped (about 8 tablespoons)
Salt and freshly ground black pepper to taste
3 pints (1½ litres) water
1 bag dashi (Japanese soup stock)*
1 lb (500 g) wholewheat noodles

Skin and bone the chicken, then cut the meat into shreds. Mix the shreds with the cornflour, then stir-fry, in the groundnut oil, over a high heat until cooked through. Add the soy sauce, sesame oil, sherry, spring onions, and salt and pepper and stir-fry briefly. Set aside.

Meanwhile, bring the water to the boil in a large saucepan. Add the dashi bag and simmer for 20 minutes. At the same time, boil the wholewheat noodles *al dente* (see page 26). Drain, then add to the stock along with the chicken mixture and serve.

Fried Thai Noodles

The addition of broccoli to the traditional Thai noodle dish improves it in both texture and colour. You might try other vegetables as well.

1 lb (500 g) wide, flat noodles
2 teaspoons sesame oil*
2 tablespoons groundnut oil, more if necessary
2 cloves garlic, peeled and sliced
8 oz (250 g) shredded, cooked chicken or prawns
3 tablespoons crushed yellow beans*
2 tablespoons fish sauce,* or to taste
Salt and freshly ground black pepper to taste
8 oz (250 g) broccoli florets

Chicken or beef stock as needed	1 teaspoon granulated sugar
Soy sauce to taste	1 tablespoon cornflour mixed with
1 tablespoon rice wine vinegar*	1 tablespoon water

Boil the noodles *al dente* (see page 26), then drain, toss with the sesame oil, and cool.

Heat the oil in a wok. Add the cooled noodles and stir over a high heat until browned. Place on a serving dish and keep warm.

Add more oil to the wok, if needed, then add the garlic and stir-fry until golden. Add the chicken or prawns and stir-fry briefly.

Add the crushed yellow beans, fish sauce, and salt and pepper, and toss the broccoli in the mixture. Add just enough stock to cover, then bring to the boil and cook until the broccoli is just tender.

Add the soy sauce, vinegar, and sugar and cook till heated through, then add the cornflour mixture and stir over the heat until thick. Pour over the noodles and serve.

Cold Chicken and Celery with Soba

An adaptation of a cold Chinese chicken dish to Japanese soba noodles, also often served cold. I have also made this dish with farfalle (pasta in the shape of small bows).

3 lb (1½ kg) chicken thighs and legs	400°F (200°C), mark 6, oven for 5 minutes
2 oz (60 g) fresh ginger,* chopped	6 stalks celery, cut into thin strips
3 slivers lemon rind	4 tablespoons sesame paste*
1 lb (500 g) soba noodles*	2 tablespoons rice wine vinegar*
4 tablespoons sesame oil*	1 tablespoon light soy sauce
1 tablespoon sesame seeds, parched on a baking sheet in a	1 tablespoon lemon juice
	Tabasco to taste

Place chicken pieces in a large saucepan and add the ginger and lemon rind. Cover with cold water, then bring to the boil and simmer, covered, for 40 minutes. Let cool in the liquid.

Poach the celery strips in boiling water for 2 minutes, then drain and chill.

Boil the soba noodles *al dente* (see page 26), then drain and toss with 2 tablespoons of the sesame oil and the sesame seeds. Chill.

Bone, skin, and shred the chicken. Arrange chicken and celery over the noodles, then combine the remaining ingredients, including the rest of the sesame oil, and add to the noodle mixture just before serving.

Korean Cold Noodles

This is similar to the two Korean *kuksoo bibim* meat dishes (see pages 155–6), but served cold in a way that is good for summer. The cooled chicken stock should not have jelled: if it does jell add just enough warm water, beating with a whisk, to liquefy it.

2 whole chicken breasts

4 tablespoons plus 1 teaspoon soy sauce

1 tablespoon chopped spring onions, both green part and white

1 tablespoon sesame seeds, toasted in a dry pan and ground with pestle and mortar

2 teaspoons sesame oil*

1 clove garlic, very finely chopped

Salt and freshly ground black pepper to taste

½ tin (7 oz (220 g) size) Szechuan cabbage pickles*

1½ teaspoons granulated sugar

2 eggs

1 lb (500 g) soba noodles*

Cayenne pepper to taste

Skin the chicken breasts, then place in a saucepan and add enough water to cover. Bring to the boil and simmer for 15 or 20 minutes, or until just cooked through. Cool in the liquid for 1 hour, then remove; reserve the liquid, letting it cool.

Bone the chicken, then cut the meat into thin strips, or pull apart with the fingers. Combine with 2 tablespoons of the soy sauce, the spring onions, the sesame seeds, 1 teaspoon of the sesame oil, the garlic, salt and pepper, the cabbage pickle, and 1 teaspoon of the sugar and set aside.

Beat the eggs together with the 1 teaspoon soy sauce, ½ teaspoon sugar and salt to taste. Make 'pancakes' in an oiled, heated frying pan; don't let them brown. Cool and slice into thin strips.

In a large saucepan of boiling water, cook the noodles *al dente* (see page 26). Drain immediately, run cold water over them, and drain again. After cooling the noodles, toss them with the remaining soy sauce, sesame oil, and sugar and the cayenne pepper.

Chill. Just before serving, divide the noodles between 6 serving bowls and top with the chicken mixture. Pour the reserved (cooled) liquid over the noodles to fill the bowls, and garnish with egg pancake strips.

Malay Chicken with Vermicelli

The curry powder for this dish is not packaged, but made up from an assortment of cumin, coriander, chillies, fenugreek, turmeric, and fennel seeds – in unmeasured proportions. My own mixture involves these ingredients in the following proportions:

2 oz (60 g) coriander seeds
2 oz (60 g) cumin seeds
4 to 6 dried red chillies*
2 oz (60 g) ground turmeric
½ oz (15 g) ground cinnamon

3 teaspoons ground cloves
2 oz (60 g) ground fenugreek
Seeds from 3 cardomom pods, pounded in a mortar

All of the above – heated until the mixture is aromatic in a dry heavy frying pan, and ground in a mortar or blender until pulverized – can be kept for a week or so, tightly covered, without losing much flavour. It is best to grind the mixture just before you need it, however.

2½ oz (75 g) butter, clarified (see note below)
5 large onions, diced finely and then mashed or put in the blender
4 medium tomatoes, peeled and cut in small pieces (see note on page 49)
1 small chicken, boned, with the meat cut into small pieces

1 tablespoon salt
1 tablespoon chilli powder
5 cloves garlic, diced finely and then mashed or put in the blender
1 tablespoon finely diced fresh ginger*
2 tablespoons (or more to taste) of the spice mixture (see above)
Juice of 1 lime

¼ pint (125 ml) water
1 lb (500 g) vermicelli

Parsley or fresh coriander leaves
for garnish

Heat the butter in a large, heavy saucepan. Add the mashed onion and sauté, stirring, until browned. Add the tomatoes and fry for 1 minute, stirring well, then add the chicken and stir-fry for 2 minutes, until the meat becomes firm.

Add the salt, chilli powder, garlic, ginger, and spice mixture and stir. Add a little water and stir as the mixture cooks over a low heat, for about 10 minutes. Add the lime juice and water and let boil for about 5 minutes.

Boil the noodles *al dente* (see page 26) and drain well. Toss the chicken mixture with the noodles, garnish with the parsley or coriander, and serve immediately.

Note: To clarify butter, heat it gently until it melts, then continue to heat slowly, without browning, until all bubbling stops (this shows all the water has evaporated). Remove from the heat and let it stand for a few minutes for the salt and sediment to settle, then gently pour off the fat.

Szechuan Noodles

This dish has two sauces, one tossed with the noodles, one used as a dipping sauce.

Noodle Mixture

12 oz (375 g) spaghetti
1 whole chicken breast
1 tablespoon groundnut oil

1 teaspoon sesame oil*
2 tablespoons Szechuan preserved
vegetable,* diced

Sauce I

1½ tablespoons groundnut oil
½ teaspoon chilli paste with
garlic*

1 rounded tablespoon peanut
butter
½ teaspoon sesame oil*

Sauce II

3 tablespoons soy sauce	1 pinch salt
2 tablespoons white wine vinegar	1 tablespoon sesame oil*

Throw the spaghetti into boiling water. When it rises to the top, add ½ pint (250 ml) cold water; when it rises again, add another ½ pint (250 ml). At the third rise, drain the noodles and let them cool in a container of cold water. Taste; they should be done.

Place the chicken breast in cold water in a saucepan and bring to the boil. Let simmer for 5 to 8 minutes, or until cooked through. Remove and cool.

Place the drained noodles in a large bowl and toss with the ground-nut oil, sesame oil, and Szechuan preserved vegetable. Skin the chicken and pull into shreds. Place on top of the noodles.

For Sauce I, place the groundnut oil, chilli paste, and peanut butter in a cold wok and turn the heat on to high. Reduce to medium, then stir in the sesame oil. Stir-fry for 2 minutes, then pour over the noodles and chicken. Toss.

For Sauce II, combine the ingredients and serve with noodles.

Chinese Hot Pot

An absorbing dish to eat, with no advance work besides the cutting up and arrangement of ingredients. Like the Japanese *mizutaki*, hot pot, or *hor gwo*, is a diner participation dish, each person picking out morsels from a central simmering soup. In some versions each person selects raw ingredients from a dish and holds them in the soup while they cook. In Singapore, Chinese restaurants set up tables on the pavements, each with a simmering pot in the centre, into which skewers of fish, chicken, meat, and vegetables are dumped to cook. In all versions, diners have dipping sauces for their food, and when all is cooked and eaten, the noodles and soup are poured into each person's bowl as a last 'course'. For the cooking utensil you can use a Chinese hot pot, which has a central chimney using hot coals and a moat around it for the simmering soup, an electric frying pan or electric casserole, which you can place in the centre of a table and maintain at a simmer, or a cooking pot heated over a small spirit lamp.

Soup

3 pints (1½ litres) chicken stock, approximately
2 thin slices fresh ginger*

1 teaspoon sesame oil*
½ teaspoon salt

Hot Pot Ingredients

8 oz (250 g) raw chicken, beef, or lamb, thinly sliced
8 oz (250 g) raw sea bass or other firm fish; and/or peeled prawns, and/or scallops and squid, cleaned, sliced, and parboiled; and/or 4 oz (125 g) calf's liver
1 tin or packet Chinese fishballs about 10),* drained

1 square fresh bean curd,* cubed

2 eggs, beaten with ½ teaspoon soy sauce and ½ teaspoon sugar, then fried without browning in a 'pancake', cooled, and cut into slices

1 medium lettuce, shredded

2 oz (60 g) raw spinach, shredded

4 oz (125 g) fresh bean sprouts

Leaves of 1 medium bunch watercress

4 oz (125 g) fresh mushrooms, sliced

6 dried mushrooms,* soaked in warm water for 15 minutes, then drained and sliced

1 tin hard-boiled quail eggs,* drained

1 bunch spring onions, sliced

4 oz (125 g) cellophane noodles* or very fine Chinese egg noodles,* both soaked in warm water

Dipping Sauce

Soy sauce

Chilli paste with garlic

Rice wine vinegar*

Sesame paste (tahini)*

Granulated sugar

Arrange all the ingredients on dishes or in sections of the cooking utensil. In the latter case, simply pour the stock – which has been heated with the ginger, sesame oil, and salt for 10 minutes and strained – into the pot over the ingredients. Keep at a simmer for a few minutes before eating.

If a more leisurely version is desired, heat the stock with the ginger, sesame oil, and salt and have each diner choose his ingredients and cook them. Each guest can make a dipping sauce by combining the soy sauce, chilli paste with garlic, vinegar, sugar, and sesame paste to taste, and dip each cooked ingredient in it before eating.

When everyone has finished eating, add the noodles to the soup and heat through. Serve the soup and noodles to each diner.

Mizutaki

Mizutaki is the Japanese version of the Chinese hot pot (see page 185 for directions). The Japanese version tends to be simpler, but the big difference is in the dipping sauce. The Chinese dip is spicy and oily, while the Japanese is strong with biting horseradish and tangy with lemon.

Hot Pot Ingredients

3 pints (1½ litres) clear chicken stock

1 small chicken, boned and cut into chunks; or ½ chicken and 12 oz (375 g) firm white fish, cut into small chunks; or all fish

2 squares bean curd,* cut into 1-inch (2- or 3-cm) cubes

4 large dried mushrooms,* soaked in warm water for 15 minutes, then drained and sliced

1 small head Chinese cabbage,* shredded

8 spring onions, shredded

3 carrots, scraped and cut into thin slices on a slant

4 oz (125 g) shirataki (bean thread) noodles,* soaked and drained

Sauce I

1 small daikon (long white horseradish),* grated

½ teaspoon wasabi powder*

4 tablespoons Japanese soy sauce (Kikkoman brand)

1 teaspoon lemon juice

Sauce II

Lemon juice mixed with soy sauce, to taste

Arrange all ingredients to be cooked on a serving dish.

Heat the stock in a cooking pot over a spirit lamp or electric frying pan in the middle of the table. Add salt to taste.

Each diner cooks ingredients as wanted for 2 minutes or so, and then dips in sauce before eating.

When all the meat, fish, and vegetables are eaten, add the noodles to the pot and raise heat. Cook for 2 minutes, then divide the soup and noodles among the diners' bowls.

Chilli Chicken with Noodles

Chinese quick-cooked dishes are very popular in Indian cities, and are often adapted to Indian tastes, like the following 'chilli chicken', which is a version of a recipe recently directed to Delhi housewives. This is a very hot dish, so reduce the number of chillies if you prefer.

1 small chicken or 2 whole chicken breasts, boned and cut into 1-inch (2- or 3-cm) chunks
2 teaspoons salt
$\frac{1}{4}$ teaspoon cayenne pepper
$\frac{1}{2}$ teaspoon freshly ground black pepper
1 egg white
2 tablespoons cornflour
8 tablespoons groundnut oil

1 large onion, chopped
6 cloves garlic, finely chopped
6 fresh green chillies, seeded, peeled, and finely chopped
2 tablespoons finely chopped fresh ginger*
8 large, fresh mushrooms, sliced
1 large cucumber, peeled, seeded, and cut into 1-inch (2- or 3-cm) cubes

1 tablespoon vinegar   1 lb (500 g) spaghetti boiled *al*
1 tablespoon soy sauce   *dente* (see page 26) and drained
1 teaspoon granulated sugar

Combine the chicken chunks with 1 teaspoon of the salt, the cayenne
and black peppers, the egg white, and the flour.

Heat the oil in a frying pan and fry the chicken, a few pieces at a
time, until all are done. Remove the chicken and all but 2 tablespoons
of the oil from the frying pan.

Reheat the oil and stir-fry the onion, garlic, chillies, and ginger
for 3 minutes. Add the mushrooms and cucumber and stir for 1
minute more, then add the chicken and heat through. Add the
remaining teaspoon salt, the vinegar, the sugar, and the soy sauce.

Serve over the spaghetti.

Noodles with Curried Chicken

Though my own invention, this dish is closest to a Southeast Asian
noodle curry, for the method of cooking is similar to Chinese stir-
frying while the ingredients are 'Indian'. Try health food shops or
Chinese shops for raw cashews.

1 tablespoon mustard oil* or corn oil

1 onion, finely chopped

1 tablespoon finely chopped fresh ginger

1 teaspoon each fennel seeds, cumin, coriander, and turmeric, ground or pounded with a mortar and pestle

2 small dried red chillies,* pounded

3 chicken leg quarters, boned and

sliced into 2-inch-long (5-cm) shreds

½ pint (250 ml) water, more if necessary

1 tablespoon cornflour mixed with 2 tablespoons water

1 lb (500 g) vermicelli or very thin egg noodles

Large handful raw cashews

2 tablespoons chopped parsley or fresh coriander

Heat the oil until it smokes in a large, heavy frying pan. Add the onion, then reduce the heat slightly to sauté until golden. Add the ginger and cook, stirring, for 2 minutes. Add all the spices and cook, stirring, for a minute longer.

Add the chicken and cook, stirring, until the shreds separate, then add the water and stir until it comes to the boil. Lower the heat to a simmer and cover the frying pan. Let cook for about 15 minutes. (If the water has boiled away in that time, add more. It should still be covering the chicken when it is done.)

Stir up the cornflour mixture and add to the chicken, stirring as it cooks and thickens. Cover and keep warm while preparing the noodles.

In a large pot of boiling water, cook the vermicelli until just tender, about 5 to 7 minutes. Drain well and place in a serving bowl.

Add the raw cashews to the chicken and toss well, then put the chicken mixture in the centre of the bed of noodles. Garnish the whole with the chopped parsley or coriander and serve.

Poule au Pot à la Crème

A *poule au pot*, or poached chicken, is excellent served on a bed of broad egg noodles to absorb the juices and bits of vegetables. Even better when, as in this recipe, the sauce is bound with thickened cream.

1 chicken (4 lb (2 kg)) left whole
1½ oz (45 g) butter
1 tablespoon olive oil
3 carrots, scraped and sliced
2 turnips, peeled and sliced
3 medium onions, sliced
2 stalks celery, chopped
Salt and freshly ground black
  pepper to taste

½ teaspoon dried thyme
8 tablespoons dry white wine or
  vermouth
1 bay leaf
¾ pint (375 ml) water
1 lb (500 g) broad egg noodles
½ pint (250 ml) double cream

In a heavy casserole, brown the chicken on all sides in 1 oz (30 g) of the butter and the oil. Add all the vegetables and sauté for 3 minutes, then add salt and pepper, the thyme, the wine or vermouth and the bay leaf and simmer for 2 minutes. Add the water and cover. Simmer for 1 hour or until the chicken is tender. Remove the chicken to a serving dish and keep warm.

Boil the noodles *al dente* (see page 26), then drain and toss with the remaining butter.

Meanwhile, raise the heat under the chicken cooking liquid and reduce it by half. Add the cream and boil very quickly, stirring, until it begins to thicken slightly. Taste for seasoning.

Place the noodles around the chicken and pour the sauce over all.

Moroccan Chicken Tagine
with Soup Pasta

Since couscous, the North African steamed grain dish, is one of my favourites, I particularly wanted some adaptation of it to noodles. The very fine acini di pepe, or 'peppercorn' soup pasta, do very well in this dish – and, besides, are much simpler in preparation than couscous, which must be soaked, steamed, dried, and resteamed before eating.

1 chicken, cut into small serving
  pieces
4 cloves garlic, crushed

1 tablespoon coarse kosher salt
Juice of 2 limes
1 tablespoon ground ginger

1 teaspoon freshly ground black pepper
1 teaspoon hot paprika
1 teaspoon ground turmeric
4 tablespoons chopped chives
1 teaspoon ground cinnamon
1 large bunch spring onions, chopped (about 12 tablespoons)
1½ oz (45 g) margarine
1 large onion, thinly sliced

2–3 oz (60–90 g) raisins
1 lb (500 g) dried chick-peas, soaked overnight and cooked until tender, or 3 cans (14 oz (440 g) each) chick-peas
1 lb (500 g) acini di pepe ('peppercorn' soup pasta) or large egg pastina
Harissa (red pepper paste) optional

Place the chicken pieces in a glass or ceramic bowl and toss with the garlic, salt, lime juice, ginger, and pepper. Refrigerate overnight.

Place the chicken and marinade in a heavy casserole. Add the paprika, turmeric, chives, cinnamon, and spring onions to the casserole and add enough water to cover the chicken. Simmer for 1 hour, then remove the chicken pieces, set aside, and keep warm.

Continue to simmer the stock, while adding the margarine, onion, raisins, and chick-peas, until the sauce reduces somewhat and is thicker. Taste for seasoning, then add the chicken and heat through.

Meanwhile, boil the soup pasta or pastina for about 8 minutes and drain well. Mound the pasta in a large serving bowl and toss with a few spoons of sauce. Make a well in the centre and spoon in the chicken and sauce. Serve with harissa, if desired.

Garlic Chicken with Noodles

Do not be worried by the amount of garlic; when it stews for a long time, garlic loses its strength and becomes nutty rather than pungent. My guess is that the taste will no longer be definably 'garlicky' to the uninitiated.

3 tablespoons olive oil
3 lb (1½ kg) chicken thighs and legs, cut into chunks, bones and all

4 to 5 heads garlic, cloves separated and peeled (see note below)
2 bay leaves

1 tablespoon dried tarragon
8 tablespoons chopped fresh
  parsley
½ teaspoon ground cinnamon
Salt and freshly ground black
  pepper to taste

½ pint (250 ml) dry white wine
1 lb (500 g) egg noodles
1 oz (30 g) buttered breadcrumbs
  (see note on page 58)

Preheat the oven to 375°F (190°C), mark 5.

Heat the oil in a heavy saucepan, then put in the chicken, along with the garlic, bay leaves, tarragon, parsley, cinnamon, salt, pepper, and wine. Cover tightly and simmer for 1 hour, stirring occasionally and adding a little water, if necessary.

Meanwhile, boil the egg noodles *al dente* (see page 26) and drain. Mix with the chicken and place in a buttered casserole. Top with the breadcrumbs and bake for 30 minutes, or until the crumbs brown.

Note: If you place a garlic clove on a board and smack it with the side of a cleaver, it will loosen the skin. Or drop the cloves in boiling water for 10 seconds to loosen the skins.

Avgolemono Chicken with Noodles

Avgolemono sauce, the classic Greek egg-lemon sauce, is served with many dishes – from stuffed vine leaves to baked lamb with artichokes to grilled fish. Chicken and endive are particularly good 'bound' with *avgolemono*.

1½ oz (45 g) butter
1 tablespoon vegetable oil
2 medium onions, chopped
1 bunch spring onions, chopped
  (about 8 tablespoons)
1 broiler chicken, cut into small
  chunks, bones and all
1 head endive, washed and
  chopped
½ pint (250 ml) dry white wine

1 teaspoon dried tarragon
Salt and freshly ground black
  pepper to taste
1 lb (500 g) egg noodles
4 egg yolks
4 tablespoons lemon juice
1 tablespoon grated lemon rind
1 teaspoon cornflour mixed with
  2 teaspoons cold water, if
  necessary

Heat the butter and oil in a heavy saucepan, over a medium heat. Sauté the onions and spring onions until brown, then add the endive and stir until wilted. Add the chicken and raise the heat a little, stirring as the pieces brown slightly. Add the wine, tarragon, salt, and pepper and cover the pan. Lower the heat to a simmer and cook for 20 minutes, then remove the chicken pieces.

Boil the noodles *al dente* (see page 26) and drain. Place in a warm serving dish.

Heat the chicken cooking liquid. Combine the egg yolks, lemon juice and lemon rind in a bowl and mix with a little of the hot liquid, whisking. Pour the contents of the bowl into the saucepan and stir over a very low heat as the sauce thickens. (If the sauce doesn't thicken enough, add the cornflour mixture and stir over a low heat.) Season with salt and pepper, then put the chicken on the bed of noodles and pour the sauce over all.

Poulet au Saffron

The combination of saffron and cinnamon is a key to the origin of this dish. It probably came to France from North Africa, via Spain.

1 chicken 3 lb (1½ kg), cut into small serving pieces
1 tablespoon salt
½ tablespoon freshly ground black pepper
1 oz (30 g), butter
2 tablespoons olive oil
8 ozs (250 g), fresh mushrooms, sliced
10 small white onions, peeled (see note below)
¼ teaspoon ground cinnamon
2 cloves garlic, very finely chopped
½ reaspoon dried thyme
8 tablespoons white wine or vermouth
8 tablespoons water
1 lb (500 g) flat egg noodles
¼ teaspoon saffron
½ pint (250 ml) sour cream (or crème fraîche if you have it)

Rub the chicken with the salt and pepper. Heat the butter and oil in a heavy casserole, then brown the chicken pieces. Add the mushrooms, onions, and cinnamon and cook, stirring, over a medium heat for 5 minutes. Add the garlic, thyme, wine, and water, then bring to the boil and simmer, covered, for 30 minutes, or until the chicken is tender but not falling from the bone.

Boil the egg noodles *al dente* (see page 26). Drain well and place in a large, deep serving bowl.

Combine the saffron and sour cream and stir into the chicken. Heat, but do not allow to boil.

Serve the chicken on top of the noodles.

Note: If you drop onions into boiling water for 10 seconds, the skins come off easily.

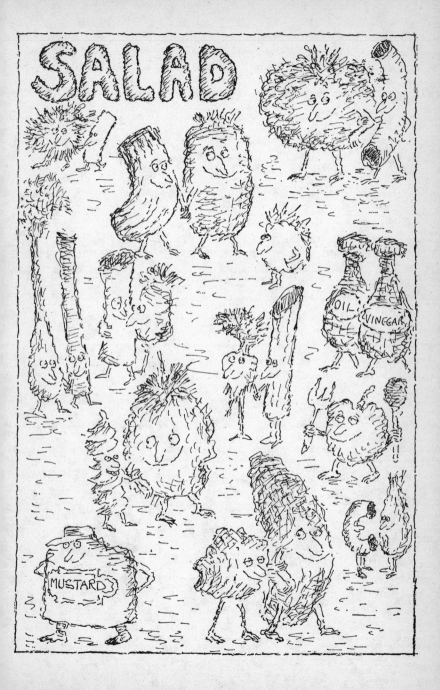

SALADS AND SIDE DISHES

Pasta and White Bean Salad

Like *pasta e fagioli*, this salad has a good nutritional balance. It is also quite fresh tasting, with its variety of fresh herbs. With this dish, never be tempted to use tinned beans.

8 oz (250 g) dried white pea beans or haricot beans
8 oz (250 g) small macaroni
1 clove garlic, very finely chopped
3 tablespoons very finely chopped fresh herbs (chives, tarragon, parsley, etc.)

6 tablespoons olive oil
1 tablespoon wine vinegar
1 teaspoon dry mustard
Salt and freshly ground black pepper to taste
Pinch of granulated sugar

Soak the beans overnight, then boil until tender but not mushy. Drain and cool.

Boil the macaroni *al dente* (see page 26). Drain and cool under running water, then toss with the beans, garlic, and herbs. Chill.

Combine the oil, vinegar, mustard, salt, pepper, and sugar and pour over the salad. Toss and serve.

New Potato Salad with Pasta

New potatoes are a seasonal treat I look forward to each year. Don't try this salad without them.

3 medium new potatoes, scrubbed
4 oz (125 g) small elbow macaroni
3 tablespoons chopped spring onions
Salt and freshly ground black pepper to taste

Generous $\frac{1}{4}$ pint (250 ml) freshly made mayonnaise (see below), thinned with a little lemon juice
Chopped fresh mint for garnish

Boil the potatoes until just tender. Skin while hot (cool just until you can touch them) and slice into a serving bowl.

Meanwhile, boil the pasta *al dente* (see page 26), drain well, and add to the bowl. Toss with the spring onions, salt, pepper, and mayonnaise.

Chill until serving time, then garnish with mint and serve.

Fresh Blender Mayonnaise

1 large egg	2 tablespoons lemon juice
½ teaspoon dry mustard	8 fl oz (200 ml) olive oil
½ teaspoon salt	

Break egg into blender. Add salt, mustard, and lemon juice, and 4 tablespoons of the oil. Cover and blend low speed. Uncover and add remaining oil in a slow stream, continuing to blend at low speed. The mayonnaise will be fairly thick. Makes about ½ pint (250 ml).

Spiced Orzo Salad

Orzo is very small, rice-shaped pasta and a good rice substitute. This is a version, in fact, of my favourite rice salad.

8 oz (250 g) orzo	2 oz (60 g) dried apricots, chopped
1 tablespoon finely shredded fresh ginger*	4 tablespoons olive oil
Freshly ground black pepper	3 tablespoons lemon juice
2 oz (60 g) raisins, chopped (cut with a floured knife to keep from sticking)	3 spring onions, chopped
	2 tablespoons chopped fresh coriander or parsley

Boil the orzo *al dente* (see page 26), then drain and cool under running water. Place in a serving bowl and add the ginger, pepper, chopped raisins and apricots, olive oil, and lemon juice. Chill.

Just before serving, toss with the spring onions and coriander or parsley.

Wianno Noodles

This is a chicken salad enlivened with fresh peppers and fresh herbs.

Salad

8 oz (250 g) elbow macaroni
8 oz (250 g) cooked, cubed boneless chicken, tossed with 2
tablespoons good mayonnaise
(see page 200 for mayonnaise
recipe)

3 tablespoons chopped red onion
1½ sweet green peppers, chopped
1 teaspoon granulated sugar
Salt and pepper to taste

Vinaigrette Dressing

3 tablespoons olive oil
1 tablespoon wine vinegar
2 cloves garlic, very finely
chopped

4 tablespoons finely chopped
fresh dill or basil, or ½ teaspoon
dried

Boil the noodles *al dente* (see page 26), then drain and cool under running water.

Combine the ingredients for the vinaigrette dressing, then toss the noodles in it. Add the chicken, onion, peppers, sugar, salt, and pepper. Mix well and serve immediately, or refrigerate to serve later. (This salad is better chilled.)

Herb Macaroni Salad

This recipe gives you a chance to choose your own flavourings. Several combinations are good – for instance, I like tarragon and chives. But fresh herbs only, please.

1 lb (500 g) elbow or farfallette
macaroni
3 tablespoons chopped fresh
herbs (parsley, basil, dill, tarragon, thyme, chives, fennel,
sorrel, savory, mint, etc.)

1 large sweet red pepper, seeded
and sliced
Salt and freshly ground black
pepper to taste
¾ pint (375 ml) good mayonnaise,
thinned slightly with tarragon

vinegar (see page 200 for mayonnaise recipe)

4 hard-boiled eggs, sliced, for garnish

2 tablespoons chopped fresh parsley for garnish

Boil the macaroni *al dente* (see page 26), then drain and cool under running water. Toss with the remaining ingredients, except for the garnishes, then place in a serving dish and chill.

Serve, garnished with the hard-boiled eggs and parsley.

Avocado–Prawn Noodles

An unusual version of prawn salad that would be excellent as an hors d'oeuvre or first course, with a few radishes and black olives to garnish.

1 lb (500 g) prawns, peeled

2 ripe avocados, peeled and cut into 1-inch (2- or 3-cm) slices

Garlic Vinaigrette Dressing (page 229)

12 oz (375 g) small elbow macaroni

3 tablespoons chopped parsley

mixed with a little fresh basil | Olive oil and lemon juice as
or thyme | needed

Marinate the avocado and prawns in garlic vinaigrette dressing for
about 30 minutes.

Boil the macaroni *al dente* (see page 26), then drain and cool under
running water. Toss the macaroni with the prawn and avocado
mixture, then top with the chopped parsley mixture. Add olive oil
and lemon juice to taste and serve.

Indian Salad

Cooked pork, marinated in a sharp vinaigrette and then combined
with macaroni tossed in curried mayonnaise, makes a good luncheon
dish. You might also use cold chicken, turkey, prawns, or veal. And,
if you prefer, cos lettuce leaves may be used as a base for the salad.

Vinaigrette Dressing

4 tablespoons olive oil
2 tablespoons white wine vinegar
2 tablespoons very finely chopped
  chives

1 teaspoon dry mustard
Salt and freshly ground black
  pepper to taste

Salad

1 lb (500 g) lean cooked pork,
  shredded
2 cucumbers, peeled, cut lengthwise, seeded, and cut into thin
  strips
1 tablespoon coarse salt
8 oz (250 g) macaroni, cooked *al
  dente* (see page 26), drained,
  and chilled

8 tablespoons freshly made
  mayonnaise, mixed with 2 teaspoons imported curry powder,
  preferably Madras (see page
  200 for mayonnaise recipe)
Chopped spring onions or fresh
  coriander for garnish

Mix the vinaigrette ingredients and marinate the pork in them for
1 hour.

Combine the cucumber with the salt and set aside for 30 minutes. Drain and pat dry, then combine with the pork, macaroni, and mayonnaise.

Mound the salad, garnish with the spring onions or coriander, and serve.

Chicken Salad with Grapes

An interesting 'Roquefort' style dressing for chicken, nuts, grapes, and noodles. Toss it all together just at the last minute.

Salad

12 oz (375 g) egg noodles
3 large whole chicken breasts, roasted or simmered in stock or water until firm
3 oz (90 g) almond flakes, toasted in ½ oz (15 g) butter until golden (do not let burn)

1 lb (500 g) seedless green grapes, washed and stems removed
2 spring onions, chopped
1 oz (30 g) blue cheese, crumbled

Dressing

4 oz (125 g) blue cheese
2 tablespoons lemon juice, or more to taste
4 tablespoons olive oil or mayonnaise

Salt and freshly ground black pepper to taste
1 tablespoon fresh dill or 1 teaspoon dried dillweed

Boil the noodles *al dente* (see page 26), then drain, run under cold water, and chill.

Shred the chicken into 1-inch (2- or 3-cm) strips, then combine with the almonds, grapes, spring onions and crumbled blue cheese.

Place all the dressing ingredients in the blender and blend until smooth.

Place the noodles and chicken mixture in a serving bowl and top with the dressing. Toss well and serve.

Mauna Loa Seafood Salad

This mixture of exotic tastes tossed with cold penne or cut macaroni is a main-course salad.

Dressing

1 shallot, very finely chopped
1 clove garlic, very finely chopped
Generous ½ pint (250 ml) good
  mayonnaise (see page 200 for
  mayonnaise recipe)
3 tablespoons chilli sauce

2 spring onions, both green part
  and white, finely chopped
1 teaspoon Worcestershire sauce
¼ teaspoon Tabasco
½ teaspoon dry mustard

Salad

1 lb (500 g) large prawns, peeled
1 lb (500 g) cooked crabmeat,
  shredded
2 avocados, peeled and sliced
2 tins (11 oz (340 g) each) mandarin oranges, drained
1 lb (500 g) penne or cut macaroni, boiled *al dente* (see page

26), then drained and cooled
  under running water
4 oz (125 g) macadamia nuts,
  roughly cracked, if you can get
  them
4 oz (125 g) pecans, roughly
  cracked

Mix all dressing ingredients together. Toss with the prawns, crab, avocados, mandarin oranges, and noodles, then chill for 2 hours. Just before serving, toss with the macadamia nuts and pecans.

Bean Sprout Salad with Noodles

A very good salad to accompany grilled food, like chicken *yakitori* or grilled fish. Use only fresh bean sprouts (easily grown in your kitchen) – tinned sprouts are soggy and have a poor flavour.

6 oz (180 g) bean thread noodles*
3 oz (90 g) fresh bean sprouts
3 spring onions, chopped

2 tablespoons dried shrimp,*
  which has been soaked in warm
  water for 15 minutes (optional)

2 tablespoons rice wine vinegar*
2 tablespoons soy sauce
1 teaspoon granulated sugar

1 teaspoon sesame oil*
Salt and freshly ground black pepper to taste

Soak the bean thread noodles in hot water for 10 minutes, then drain and place under running water to cool.

Wash the bean sprouts, then drain. Toss with the cooled noodles, spring onions, and dried shrimp.

Combine the remaining ingredients, toss with the bean sprout mixture, and serve.

Small Bows with Beans and Tuna

A very nice appetizer or part of an antipasto. You can give this salad an interesting 'bite' by stirring a small amount of harissa, a red pepper paste from North Africa, into the dressing, thus making it resemble the Tunisian salad called *méchouia*.

4 oz (125 g) small pasta bows (farfalle or farfallette)
1 purple onion, thinly sliced
6 oz (190 g) small white beans, soaked overnight and boiled until tender *but not mushy* (2 or 3 hours for old beans)
Salt and freshly ground black pepper to taste

Garlic Vinaigrette Dressing (page 229)
1 tin (7 oz (220 g)) tuna, drained and separated into rough chunks
1 sweet red pepper, seeded and sliced into very thin strands

Boil the pasta *al dente* (see page 26). Drain and cool under running water, then toss with the onions, beans, salt, pepper, and dressing. Mound the tuna on top, decorate with strands of red pepper, and serve.

Antipasto Noodles

This is a kind of one-pot antipasto in which pasta serves as a base for contrasting tastes, such as spicy sausage, tangy cheese, and sardines. You could add olives, marinated mushrooms, or any other cold salad ingredient.

1 lb (500 g) noodles
4 oz (125 g) feta cheese
2 oz (60 g) peperoni* slices, chopped
½ cucumber, peeled and sliced
2 hard-boiled eggs

1 tin sardines
Salt and freshly ground pepper to taste
Garlic Vinaigrette Dressing (page 229)

Cook the noodles *al dente* (see page 26). Drain and run under cold water.

Mix the cheese and peperoni into the noodles, then lay slices of cucumber, hard-boiled egg, and sardines on top of the mixture. Season with salt and pepper, top with the dressing and serve.

Tossed Salad with Garlic Noodles

Pasta here is like garlic croutons for salad; it is deep-fried after being marinated with garlic. This garnish can be used for other dishes – for topping gratinées, and so forth.

Salad

¾ pint (375 ml) corn oil
4 oz (125 g) spaghettini or ordinary spaghetti, broken into 2-inch (5-cm) strips and cooked *al dente* (see page 26)
½ head cos lettuce
Equal amount of carefully washed

fresh spinach leaves, tough stems removed
8 oz (250 g) tomatoes, sliced across
3 spring onions, chopped
3 cloves garlic, mashed well
3 tablespoons salad oil

Garlic Lemon Dressing

1 teaspoon dry mustard
1 tablespoon water
1 clove garlic, finely chopped
1 teaspoon granulated sugar

1 teaspoon salt
8 fl oz (200 ml) olive oil
3 tablespoons lemon juice
1 teaspoon grated onion (optional)

Heat the corn oil in a deep saucepan or deep-fryer to 400°F (200°C) on a deep-frying thermometer. Spread the pasta on paper towels and fry, a small amount at a time, until golden brown and crisp. Remove with a slotted spoon and drain on paper towels.

Combine the remaining salad ingredients, then sprinkle with pasta just before tossing with the garlic lemon dressing.

Note: If you do not have a thermometer test the oil with a noodle or a cube of bread; if it browns in 60 seconds it is hot enough. If the oil smokes it is too hot.

Alsatian Noodles

The simplest noodle side dish. Wonderful when made with fresh noodles, as an accompaniment to grilled dishes.

1 lb (500 g) egg noodles
3 oz (90 g) toasted breadcrumbs
6 oz (190 g) butter, cut into small
  pieces

Salt and freshly ground pepper to
  taste

Boil the noodles *al dente* (see page 26). Drain and place in a serving dish, then toss with the breadcrumbs, butter, salt and pepper.

Cold Noodles with Tahini Dressing

Tahini is ground sesame seeds, a wonderful ingredient to know. If you haven't a Middle Eastern supplier, you can grind the seed in a blender to produce tahini. It is also good with cooked vegetables, especially aubergine.

1 lb (500 g) vermicelli
3 tablespoons tahini*
2 cloves garlic, very finely
  chopped
2 tablespoons lemon juice

Salt and freshly ground pepper to
  taste
1 tablespoon water
¼ pint (125 ml) olive oil, or as
  needed

Place the tahini in a small bowl and mix in the garlic, lemon juice, salt, pepper, and water. Blend until smooth.

Gradually add the olive oil, while whisking with a fork until smooth and medium thick (as in making mayonnaise).

Boil the vermicelli *al dente* (see page 26), then drain, cool under running water, and toss with the sauce.

DESSERTS

DESSERTS, NEAR NOODLES, SAUCES, AND STUFFINGS

DESSERTS

The following is a series of 'noodle puddings' culled from several traditions. These are all sweet, but, surprisingly, not always intended as desserts. I am grateful to Eleanor Wurgaft for her suggestions.

Noodle Kugel

1 lb (500 g) broad egg noodles, boiled *al dente* (see page 26) and drained
1 lb (500 g) cottage cheese
2 oz (60 g) granulated sugar
½ teaspoon ground cinnamon

1 teaspoon vanilla essence
2 oz (60 g) butter, melted
½ pint (250 ml) milk
Raisins and nuts to taste
3 eggs, beaten
1½ oz (45 g) crushed cornflakes

Preheat the oven to 350°F (175°C), mark 4.

Combine all the ingredients except the cornflakes; add the eggs last. Butter a 9 × 13-inch (22 × 32-cm) roasting pan or casserole and add the mixture. Top with the crushed cornflakes and bake for 35 minutes.

Noodle Pudding Soufflé

8 eggs, separated
1 pint (500 ml) sour cream
8 oz (250 g) cottage cheese

¾ pint (375 ml) milk
5 oz (160 g) granulated sugar
1 teaspoon vanilla essence

8 oz (250 g) fine egg noodles,   4 oz (125 g) butter
   boiled *al dente* (see page 26) and   1 tin (16 oz (500 g)) pitted dark
   drained   cherries, drained
Grated rind of 1 lemon   ½ teaspoon ground cinnamon

Preheat the oven to 350°F (175°C), mark 4.

Combine the egg yolks, sour cream, cottage cheese, milk, sugar, and vanilla in the blender and blend until smooth.

Place the noodles in a mixing bowl and add the blended mixture and the grated lemon rind.

Beat the egg whites until stiff.

Melt the butter in a heavy casserole. Fold the egg whites into the noodle mixture and place in the casserole. Bake for 1 hour, or until puffed and brown, then remove from the oven and cool to warm. (Or let cool and reheat for 10 minutes at 350°F (175°C), mark 4.) Surround with the cherries, sprinkle with the cinnamon and serve.

Noodle Pudding with Apricots

3 oz (90 g) granulated sugar   cooked *al dente* (see page 26)
2 eggs, separated   and drained
1 teaspoon ground cinnamon   1 tin (14 oz (440 g)) apricot halves
1 oz (30 g) butter, melted   1 tin (8 oz (250 g)) crushed pine-
8 oz (250 g) broad egg noodles,   apple

Preheat the oven to 325°F (160°C), mark 3.

Combine the sugar and egg yolks and beat well. Add the cinnamon and melted butter. Beat the egg whites until stiff and fold in, together with the drained noodles.

Grease a casserole. Put in half of the noodle mixture. Drain apricot halves and crushed pineapple. Put half the fruit on top of the noodle mixture, then add the reserved half of the noodles, and top with the remaining fruit. Bake for 30 minutes, then serve.

Noodle Dairy Pudding

10 oz (310 g) medium egg noodles
½ teaspoon ground cinnamon
Salt to taste
2–3 oz (60–90 g) raisins
3 oz (90 g) granulated sugar

1 teaspoon almond essence
¾ pint (375 ml) milk
3 eggs
4 oz (125 g) butter

Preheat the oven to 350°F (175°C), mark 4.

Boil the noodles *al dente* (see page 26), then drain and run cold water through them. Place in a mixing bowl and add the cinnamon, salt, raisins, sugar, and almond essence.

Beat the milk and eggs together and add to the noodle mixture, then melt half the butter and add this to the mixture.

Heat the remaining butter in a baking dish, then pour in the noodle mixture and bake until the pudding is well browned, about 50 minutes.

Hungarian Baked Noodle Dessert

Hungarian noodle desserts are related to Jewish noodle puddings, but are more definitely desserts, and usually do not appear earlier in the meal, as do Jewish noodle puddings.

8 oz (250 g) wide noodles
1½ oz (45 g) butter
2 oz (60 g) walnuts, chopped
3 tablespoons apricot jam
Grated rind of 1 lemon

2 tablespoons breadcrumbs
½ pint (250 ml) sour cream
2 oz (60 g) granulated sugar
Icing sugar

Preheat the oven to 350°F (175°C), mark 4.

Boil the noodles *al dente* (see page 26), then drain well. Combine while warm with the butter, nuts, jam, lemon rind, breadcrumbs and granulated sugar. Stir in the sour cream, then place in a greased baking dish and bake for 30 minutes.

Dust with icing sugar and serve.

Hawaiian Banana Pudding
with Vermicelli

A dessert so sweet and rich your teeth will sing. Give small portions.

4 bananas
¾ pint (375 ml) coconut milk (see page 41)
4 tablespoons honey
1 oz (30 g) cornflour
8 tablespoons water

1 teaspoon lemon juice
4 oz (125 g) vermicelli, broken up, boiled *al dente* (see page 26) and drained
Tinned coconut cream and/or shredded coconut

Cook the bananas in the coconut milk for 15 minutes. Add the honey, then put through a sieve.

Mix the cornflour, water, and lemon juice and add to the banana mixture. Cook, stirring, as the mixture thickens, then remove from the heat and stir in the vermicelli. Chill in individual cups, then serve with coconut cream and/or garnish with shredded coconut.

Pasta Dolce

A very sweet and heavy pudding that reminds me a little of English nursery puddings. Try serving it with double cream.

8 oz (250 g) small macaroni or acini di pepe ('peppercorn' soup pasta)

1¼ pints (625 ml) milk

1½ oz (45 g) granulated sugar

1½ oz (45 g) brown sugar

¼ teaspoon fresh grated nutmeg

½ teaspoon ground cinnamon

Chopped walnuts for garnish

Boil the macaroni in the milk (being careful not to let it boil over) for 8 minutes. Add the sugars and cook for 10 more minutes, stirring. Add the nutmeg and cinnamon and serve lukewarm or hot, garnished with the chopped walnuts.

Phaluda (Cornflour Vermicelli)

These noodles are very unusual; a pale bluish white, they are not cooked in the ordinary way at all, but are merely a cornflour paste 'hardened' in cold water. I had them first in Delhi, as a bed for the remarkable rosewater frozen ice cream, *kulfi*.

3 oz (90 g) cornflour mixed with 12 fl oz (300 ml) water

Stir over a medium heat for about 12 minutes. The mixture changes from watery to very thick, then to a translucent blue colour, then loosens up just a bit.

Using a potato ricer, colander or large-holed sieve, press spoonfuls of paste into a bowl of iced water. The noodles will firm slightly into thin, translucent vermicelli bits. Keep in the water until needed, then drain and serve under almond syrup and softened vanilla ice cream, or either of the following:

Kulfi

1 large tin sweetened condensed milk
½ pint (250 ml) double cream
1½ teaspoons rosewater or vanilla essence
2 oz (60 g) blanched almonds, finely chopped (not ground in the blender)
1 oz (30 g) pistachio nuts, finely chopped
3 oz (90 g) granulated sugar
6 tablespoons water

Combine the condensed milk, cream, ½ teaspoon of the rosewater or vanilla essence, and the nuts. Stir well and freeze. During the freezing, which takes 4 hours or more, the nuts rise to the top. Add a mixture of the sugar and water boiled for 5 minutes. Then add the remaining teaspoon of rosewater and chill.

Fruits in Syrup

1 tin (11 oz (340 g)) mandarin oranges, 2 tablespoons of the syrup reserved
1 tin (8 oz (250 g)) pineapple chunks
1 small tin lychees
2 bananas, sliced
1 teaspoon lemon juice
2 tablespoons honey

Combine all the ingredients and chill.

NEAR NOODLES

Many of the recipes given in this book would be delicious with these 'not quite' noodles instead of *pasta secca* or freshly made noodles, and many of the sauces are excellent with them.

The sorts of crêpes given here are not the classic French sort (for which you can find recipes elsewhere), but a Korean pancake, which is served rolled with spiced beef shreds, spring onion, cooked egg strips, and chillies; a manicotti crêpe that is rolled with various stuffings and baked with tomato sauce; and blintzes, for cheese and meat fillings.

The other kinds of 'near noodles' are Italian gnocchi, German or Czech spaetzle, and Hungarian csipetke, all of which could also be called 'near dumplings'. They are boiled in water before being served with sauces and meats, or gratinéed with butter and cheese.

Blintzes

These 'crêpes' are most often served with a cheese filling, and with a big spoonful of sour cream on top. You could also use a minced meat filling, or a fruit filling.

2 eggs	Cheese Filling for Blintzes or
4 oz (125 g) plain flour	Kreplach (see below)
1 tablespoon groundnut oil	Butter for frying
12 fl oz (300 ml) milk	Sour cream

Beat the eggs until light, then add the flour and oil and mix until smooth. Add the milk, stirring until the batter is smooth and thin.

Heat a small (6- to 8-inch (15- to 20-cm)) frying pan and grease lightly with more oil. Pour a small ladleful (about 2 tablespoons) of batter in, tilting the pan so the batter covers the bottom. Cook until the bottom is browned, then turn carefully to brown the other side. Stack the pancakes on a plate or towel as they are finished.

Prepare the cheese filling as directed below.

To fill the blintzes, place a heaped teaspoonful of filling in the centre of each pancake. Roll the pancake up loosely, then, with the seam on the bottom, tuck the ends in.

Heat enough butter in a frying pan to coat the bottom generously, then fry the blintzes, a few at a time, until golden brown, first on the seam side, then on the top.

Serve immediately, topped with a spoonful of sour cream.

Cheese Filling for Blintzes or Kreplach

1¼ lb (625 g) cottage cheese or ricotta*	Salt and freshly ground black pepper to taste
2 eggs	1 oz (30 g) butter, melted

Combine all the ingredients and mix well until smooth.

Use in blintzes (see above) or kreplach.

Hungarian Csipetke

These are closest to spaetzle, but, because they are made by pinching the dough with the fingers, they are usually called 'pinched noodles'.

4 oz (125 g) plain flour	Water
Salt	Butter or oil
1 egg	

Place the flour and $\frac{1}{2}$ teaspoon salt in a bowl and make a well in the centre. Add the egg to the well, then enough water to make a soft dough. Knead until smooth.

Bring a saucepan of water to the boil. Add salt to taste.

Roll out the dough to about $\frac{1}{8}$ inch (3 mm) thick. Pinch off pieces about $\frac{1}{2}$ inch (1 cm) in size and drop them into the boiling water. When they rise to the surface, they are done. Drain well and toss with butter or oil before serving.

Note: These are good added to a soup after they have been boiled.

Korean Pancakes

These are similar to French crêpes, but are eaten with an interesting filling of lightly sautéed beef strips, shredded vegetables and spring onions, and a sauce of sesame seeds, garlic, soy sauce, and chopped ginger. They are a delicious substitute for the much more difficult *moo shi* pancakes served with 'mandarin' style dishes.

6 oz (190 g) plain flour	$\frac{3}{4}$ pint (375 ml) milk
2 eggs, lightly beaten	3 oz (90 g) butter, melted

Place the flour in a bowl. Beat together the remaining ingredients and add to the flour, stirring with a wire whisk.

Brush a 6-inch (15-cm) pan with butter or tasteless oil. Heat the pan and add a small ladleful of batter (about 2 tablespoons), swirling the pan so the batter covers the bottom. Cook until the crêpe is set, then cook briefly on the other side. Stack the pancakes as they are done.

These can be set aside for an hour or so, and used at room temperature.

Manicotti Crêpes

4 oz (135 g) plain flour	6 eggs
13 fl oz (325 ml) milk	Salt to taste

Place the flour in a mixing bowl. Add the milk a little at a time, while beating with a wire whisk, then add the eggs, one at a time, beating well after every addition. Add salt to taste, and strain the batter well. The batter can be set aside or refrigerated for an hour or so.

Brush a 6-inch (15-cm) pan with olive oil or butter. Heat the pan, then add batter, one ladleful (about 2 tablespoons) for each crêpe, and swirl the pan around so the batter covers the bottom. Cook just until the crêpe is set, then turn and cook very briefly on the other side.

Turn the crêpe out on to waxed paper, and cover it with a further piece of waxed paper. Then as each crêpe is made, turn it on to the pile, separating crêpes from each other with waxed paper. Use immediately, stuffed with one of the fillings on pages 230–31, or store in the refrigerator until needed. After stuffing and rolling, the crêpes can be baked with a sauce, or gratinéed with cheese under a grill.

Note: Any leftover crêpes can be saved, cut in strips and used in soups. They are very good in endive soup with grated Parmesan.

Spaetzle

The first time I ever had this was in the kitchen of a German friend, who had just completed weeks of marinating beef, searing it on a grill three floors down, and slow cooking it into the most marvellous sauerbraten I've ever had. The spaetzle were made over a huge saucepan of boiling water in a contraption that looks like a potato ricer, made just for these light, eggy dumpling strands.

Spaetzle are wonderful with much less troublesome foods than sauerbraten, however – tomato sauces, chicken livers in sour cream, a light vegetable sauce. Or you can eat them by themselves, drained, tossed with butter and cheese and put under the grill for a couple of minutes.

1 lb (500 g) plain flour	Pinch of freshly grated nutmeg
4 eggs	1 oz (30 g) butter, melted
3 tablespoons cream	
Salt and freshly ground pepper to taste	

Combine all the ingredients except the melted butter in a mixing bowl and beat well. Force through a spaetzle maker, ricer, colander or large-holed sieve – or spread out on a floured board and simply cut off ribbons of the mixture – into a saucepan of boiling, salted water. Poach for 5 minutes, then remove with a slotted spoon to a colander and drain for a minute or so. Place in a serving dish and toss with melted butter.

Variations for Spaetzle

1. Add 2 oz (60 g) chopped raw spinach to the dough before cooking.
2. Add 6 oz (190 g) very finely chopped ham to the dough before cooking.
3. Add 2–3 oz (60–90 g) grated Gruyère to the dough before cooking.
4. Toss cooked spaetzle with sauerkraut and chopped ham.
5. Toss cooked spaetzle with mushrooms sautéed in butter, place in buttered shallow casserole, sprinkle 2 tablespoons grated Parmesan on top, and bake in a 350°F (175°C), mark 4, oven until brown.

Potato Gnocchi

For a long time, I made these with only one sauce, one with chicken livers in wine, only recently to discover how good they are with many other sauces, even plain tomato sauce. They are very easy to make.

2 lb (1 kg) potatoes, peeled and
  quartered
8 oz (250 g) plain flour

2 eggs
1 oz (30 g) butter, melted
½ teaspoon salt

Boil the potatoes until tender, then drain and mash. Add the flour, eggs, and butter and season with salt. Knead until smooth (the dough should be fairly soft).

Have a large saucepan of water boiling. With a teaspoon, scoop up ½ teaspoonfuls of the dough at a time, pushing it off the spoon with another teaspoon and dropping it into the water. Let the gnocchi boil for about 3 minutes; they should float to the surface.

Remove the gnocchi with a slotted spoon and let them drain, then place them in a serving dish and toss with sauce, or with butter and cheese. They can be put under the grill with cheese, to brown. Good also with a pesto sauce (see pages 226–7 or page 67).

Semolina Gnocchi

These are made in a different way from the potato gnocchi – instead of being boiled, they are cut out of a firm dough and grilled or heated with their sauce.

½ pint (250 ml) milk
4–6 oz (125–190 g) semolina
Salt and freshly ground black
  pepper to taste

Pinch of freshly grated nutmeg
3 oz (90 g) Parmesan cheese,
  freshly grated
2 eggs

Bring the milk to the boil and stir in the semolina, salt, pepper, and nutmeg. Stir over the heat until the mixture is *very* thick, then remove from the heat and stir in the cheese. Beat in the eggs, one at a time.

Butter a baking sheet and pour the mixture on to it to a depth of about ¼ inch (½ cm). Chill, then cut the dough into rounds or small squares and place these in a greased baking dish. Heat for 20 minutes in a 325°F (160°C), mark 3 oven with sauce or cheese.

Indian Chick-pea Noodle Snack

Similar deep-fried snacks are sold everywhere in India – often brightly coloured, sometimes glistening with syrup.

8 oz (250 g) chick-pea flour*	Salt
1 teaspoon or more imported curry powder, preferably Madras	Natural yogurt as needed
	Corn oil for deep frying

Combine the flour, curry powder, and 1 teaspoon salt. Add just enough yogurt to make a paste; it should not be at all runny.

Heat oil in a deep saucepan to 350°F (175°C) on a deep-frying thermometer. Using a potato ricer, colander or large-holed sieve, force the mixture through into the hot oil, a little at a time, to make thin 'noodle shreds'. Fry until the noodles are crisp and golden.

Remove with a slotted spoon on to paper towels to drain. Toss with salt and serve as a cocktail snack.

Note: If you do not have a thermometer test the oil with a cube of bread. If it browns in 60 seconds it is hot enough. If the oil smokes it is too hot.

SAUCES

Although directions for most sauces are contained in the recipes, some reappear so often or are so basic or interesting that I include them here for reference. This will also allow you to experiment with them, and to use them in contexts different from the ones you'll find in this book.

Fresh Tomato Sauce

2 tablespoons olive oil
1 onion, finely chopped
1 clove garlic, very finely chopped
2 lb fresh tomatoes, peeled, seeded, and chopped (see note on page 49)

½ teaspoon dried thyme
1 tablespoon fresh basil or 1 teaspoon dried
Salt and freshly ground black pepper to taste
Pinch of granulated sugar

Heat the olive oil in a heavy saucepan. Sauté the onion and garlic until golden, then add the tomatoes. Add the herbs and other seasonings and let simmer until the tomatoes are soft and turning into a purée.

Put through a food mill or sieve, then back into the pan for further cooking if the sauce is not thick enough. (Makes 1–1½ pints (500–750 ml).)

Spaghetti Sauce

2 tablespoons olive oil
1 medium onion, chopped
12 oz (375 g) minced beef
1 large tin (28 oz (875 g) size) Italian plum tomatoes, plus 1 small tin (8 oz (250 g) size)
1 tin (5 oz (160 g) size) tomato paste
1 green pepper, finely chopped (optional)

8 oz (250 g) fresh mushrooms, chopped
4 tablespoons fresh basil or 2 tablespoons dried
1 tablespoon granulated sugar
Salt and freshly ground black pepper to taste

Heat the olive oil in a heavy saucepan and sauté the onion until soft. Add the meat and brown it, stirring to separate, then add the tomatoes and tomato paste, crushing the tomatoes with a wooden spoon until soft.

Add the green pepper, mushrooms, and seasonings and stir the sauce until the ingredients are thoroughly mixed. Simmer for 30 minutes before serving.

Note: This sauce improves on keeping.

Tomato Paste Sauce

1 medium onion, chopped
4 tablespoons olive oil
2 tins (5 oz (160 g) each) tomato
  paste
1 pint (500 ml) water
¼ teaspoon salt
2 cloves garlic, very finely
  chopped

Freshly ground black pepper to
  taste
½ teaspoon granulated sugar
½ teaspoon dried oregano
1 bay leaf

Sauté the onion in the olive oil until golden. Add the tomato paste, then slowly add the water to the mixture, stirring constantly. Add the remaining ingredients and simmer for 30 minutes, stirring occasionally. Remove the bay leaf before serving. (Makes 1–1½ pints (500–750 ml).)

Walnut Pesto Sauce I

This is a nice variation on the basic basil pesto. For the best pesto of the basil sort, see the recipe for Pesto Genovese, page 67.

1 oz (30 g) pine nuts
2 oz (60 g) walnuts, chopped
2 teaspoons finely chopped fresh
  basil
8 tablespoons olive oil

Salt and freshly ground black
  pepper to taste
2 oz (60 g) Parmesan cheese,
  freshly grated

Place the pine nuts, walnuts, and basil in the blender (or in a mortar) and blend or mash well. Gradually add the olive oil, blending or mashing as you do. Add salt and pepper and the Parmesan and mix well. Toss with pasta just before serving.

Walnut Pesto Sauce II

2 oz (60 g) walnuts, ground
1 large bunch fresh parsley, chopped (about 12 tablespoons)
1 oz (30 g) softened butter
3 tablespoons fine breadcrumbs

8 tablespoons olive oil
2 tablespoons double cream
Salt and freshly ground black pepper to taste

Place the walnuts and parsley in a mortar or small bowl. Add the softened butter and mash into a paste. Add the breadcrumbs and then the oil, a little at a time, and blend until the mixture is smooth. Add the cream and salt and pepper.

Dill Pesto

8 tablespoons olive oil
4 cloves garlic, very finely chopped
4 oz (125 g) roughly chopped fresh dill

Salt and freshly ground black pepper to taste
2 oz (60 g) Parmesan cheese, freshly grated

Combine all the ingredients except the Parmesan in the blender and blend well. Stir in the Parmesan and serve.

White Sauce (Bechamel, Besciamella)

1 oz (30 g) butter
1 oz (30 g) plain flour
¾ pint (375 ml) milk, scalded (heated to just below boiling point)

4 tablespoons double cream
3 egg yolks
Salt and white pepper to taste
Pinch of freshly grated nutmeg

Melt the butter in a heavy saucepan. Over a low heat, stir in the flour; continue to stir for 2 or 3 minutes. Add the milk, while you stir the mixture with a wire whisk, and simmer for 10 minutes.

Beat the cream and egg yolks together and add a little hot sauce to the mixture, whisking continually. Add the yolk mixture to the saucepan and heat without boiling. Remove from the heat and season to taste. (Makes about 1 pint (500 ml).)

Cold Sesame Sauce for Noodles

1 tablespoon sesame oil*
2 teaspoons rice wine vinegar*
2 tablespoons soy sauce
2 spring onions, finely chopped

1 teaspoon granulated sugar
2 teaspoons sesame seeds, toasted in a heavy frying pan until golden

Combine all the ingredients and beat to dissolve the sugar. Toss with bean thread or other oriental noodles.

Oyster Sauce for Noodles

1 teaspoon sesame oil*
2 cloves garlic, mashed
1 tablespoon rice wine vinegar*

½ teaspoon salt
3 tablespoons oyster sauce*
1 tablespoon soy sauce

Combine all the ingredients and heat slightly. Toss with cooked meats, vegetables, or hot, drained noodles.

Spicy Noodle Dipping Sauce
(for Chinese or Korean Noodles)

1 teaspoon chilli paste with garlic*
2 tablespoons rice wine vinegar*
2 tablespoons soy sauce

1 teaspoon granulated sugar
1 teaspoon sesame oil*

Combine all the ingredients and serve as a dipping sauce for cooked vegetables, meats, or noodles.

Garlic Vinaigrette Dressing

1 teaspoon dry mustard
1 tablespoon water
1 clove garlic, very finely chopped
1 teaspoon granulated sugar
1 teaspoon salt

8 fl oz (200 ml) olive oil
3 tablespoons lemon juice or wine vinegar
1 teaspoon freshly grated onion (optional)

Combine the mustard with the water and let stand for 10 minutes, then add the garlic, sugar, salt, and olive oil and let stand for 1 hour.

Add the lemon juice or vinegar and the onion, then pour into a screw-top jar and shake well.

Savoury Butters for Noodles

These butters can be made ahead and packed in refrigerator containers, or frozen for use with hot breads as well as with noodles. However, garlic butter should only be frozen, as it can turn rancid in the refrigerator after a day or two.

For each 2 oz (60 g) of butter add:
1 teaspoon fresh herbs; or ½ clove garlic, crushed; or 1 tablespoon parsley, finely chopped; or 1 teaspoon anchovy paste

Let the butter soften, then add your choice of herb or flavouring and blend well.

Toss 1 lb (500 g) of pasta with 2 or 3 tablespoons of flavoured butter.

STUFFINGS

The following are recipes for stuffings or fillings for manicotti crêpes or pasta large shells, cannelloni, lasagne and tortellini.

Beef-Spinach Stuffing

6 oz (190 g) cold, cooked beef, very finely chopped
1 lb (500 g) spinach, cooked and very finely chopped
3 spring onions, very finely chopped
1 egg
Salt and freshly ground black pepper to taste

Combine all the ingredients and beat well.

Veal and Pork Stuffing

2 small onions, very finely chopped
1 oz (30 g) butter
8 oz (250 g) minced veal
4 oz (125 g) minced pork
1 egg
1 clove garlic, mashed
Salt and freshly ground black pepper to taste
1 oz (30 g) Parmesan cheese, freshly grated

Heat the butter in a frying pan until melted, then add the onions and sauté until golden. Scrape into a mixing bowl and combine with all the remaining ingredients. (Caution: since this filling contains pork, be sure that the finished dish is cooked through – and if you wish to taste the mixture for seasoning before stuffing your pasta, do so by sautéing a small amount in butter.)

Ricotta-Spinach Filling

1½ oz (45 g) butter or margarine
3 medium onions, finely chopped
8 oz (250 g) fresh spinach, washed and picked over
1 lb (500 g) ricotta cheese*
1 egg
2 oz (60 g) Parmesan cheese, freshly grated
Pinch of freshly ground nutmeg
Salt and freshly ground black pepper to taste

Heat the butter in a heavy frying pan and sauté the onions until golden. Add the spinach, cover, and cook until the spinach is wilted. Remove from the heat and chop finely, then add the remaining ingredients and beat well.

Hungarian Sweet Filling for Pasta

This, in a sort of ravioli that is dusted with sugar after boiling, makes a very interesting dessert.

1 oz (30 g) semolina	$\frac{1}{2}$–$\frac{3}{4}$ pint (250–375 ml) sour cream
8 fl oz (200 ml) milk	1 egg
2 oz (60 g) granulated sugar	1 tablespoon grated lemon rind

In a small saucepan, heat the milk to simmering and cook the semolina in it for 5 minutes. Off the heat, beat in the remaining ingredients. Use in tortellini-like forms or in ravioli. Boil, drain, and serve sprinkled with sugar.

INDEX